Healing in the Hebrew Months

Book One
Second Edition

A Biblical Understanding of
Each Season's Emotional Healing

Leah Lesesne, MA

ISBN: 978-1-7357031-4-5

For bulk orders contact the author at:
leah@shelemah.com
P.O. Box 11489
Atlanta, GA 30310

Laura Hoefakker Editor

Printed in the United States

Disclaimer

Leah Lesesne is not a doctor, licensed dietitian or licensed counselor. The information in this book should not be seen as medical, nutritional, or mental health advice and is not intended to take the place of consulting licensed health care professionals. Check with your doctor, dietitian, counselor, and/or other health professional before implementing any of the suggestions outlined in this book.

Table of Contents

Introduction

Different Seasons

Ever notice how there are different seasons of life within the earth's four seasons? We notice the slight chill in the morning air near the end of summer and know that autumn is on its way. We also notice the shift in store displays and how they signal the holidays to come. Rhythms of vacation, spring cleaning, and back to school all signal something about the season we are entering into.

It should be no surprise then, that there are spiritual seasons throughout the year as well. As Ecclesiastes

3:1 (NKJV) tells us, *"To everything there is a season, a time for every purpose under heaven."* We can pursue emotional healing any time of year, but there is peace and power in synchronizing with the seasons of what God is doing at that time. One way of aligning with these rhythms of healing is the spiritual significance of the Hebrew months.

My Journey with the Hebrew Months

I've always been fascinated by Jewish culture and what we as Christians can learn from our Jewish roots. In high school I began learning Hebrew, college was packed full of Hebrew and Jewish studies electives, and for a season I even spent time as part of a Messianic congregation. Yet, somehow, I had never paid much attention to the Hebrew calendar.

My friend Seneca of Freedom Flowers introduced me to the spiritual significance in each Hebrew month through her *Times and Seasons* subscription club. As I became more aware of the passing of each month, I began to notice in my own life the shifting of spiritual seasons and the emotional healing that came easily in those times.

Paying attention to the Hebrew calendar has helped deepen my spiritual rhythms and connect me more with the heart of what God is doing in that season. It's forced me to slow down just a bit and pay more attention to not only the passing of months and days, but also the full breadth of experience in that time.

Rhythms Unnoticed

Whether or not you pay attention to the rhythms of the Hebrew months you are affected by them. When you know what to look for, you realize that when we listen to God's leading, we often are aligning exactly with what the months already signify.

One example of this is my church's move onto our property. As a church, we've owned 100 acres for a few years now but have had some setbacks and shifts in timeline for getting a building. Over the summer, the leaders felt a press to get onto the property by September –which meant moving into a tent instead of a building. Unaware, the very day they chose to move onto our property and into a tent was Rosh Hashanah, which marks the beginning of the High Holy Days including the Feast of Booths that commemorates Israel living in tents in the wilderness.

Since that Rosh Hashanah move into our tent, I've noticed that many of the sermons also align with the theme of the Hebrew month even though the speaker is unaware of those rhythms. Just like we breathe without thinking about it, we experience these shifts in season whether we recognize them or not. But just like we can purposely give attention to our breath and benefit from deep breathing, when we pay attention to the Hebrew months we can intentionally align with the theme of that season.

God, of course, moves as he pleases whenever he pleases and we certainly have access to any kind of emotional healing any time of year; but when we learn the spiritual rhythms of the Hebrew months and the emotional healing ripe for the picking, we unlock a new way of communicating with him that allows for greater revelations to follow. Instead of wondering what God is doing or saying, we can have an idea of what he's already interested in talking about in that season and join the conversation.

Where We're Headed

This book is the first in a three-part collection covering all the different facets of meaning found in the Hebrew months. In this book I cover the biblical significance of the months as well as the emotional themes. In part two Seneca of Freedom Flowers will introduce you to the tribes, stones, gates, and constellations associated with each month. And in part three, Del of Healing Frequencies Music will go deep with the letters associated with each month and the ways she has used the Hebrew alphabet to make music.

As much as possible we have used Bible references as our main source for understanding the months. We've filled in the gaps with rabbinical teachings and Jewish traditions that, while not scripture, in many cases have better preserved the history and significance of the Hebrew calendar. We also draw upon revelations God has given each of us as we've gone on this journey of understanding the Hebrew months.

Know Your Bible

When we mention biblical events and themes in scripture, we will often explain these events in context of the month, but we do expect you to have basic knowledge of the Bible. We encourage you to learn more on your own reading the Bible references we give or doing some searching to find more information about the events we mention in passing without a reference.

Messianic Jew-ish

We should also clarify to set proper expectations that while these books are listed in the "Messianic Jewish" category, there should be an emphasis on the *-ish*. None of the authors consider themselves Messianic Jewish though we have spent time with those communities and have great appreciation for them. We are not #TorahObservant. We say God instead of G-d and Jesus instead of Yeshua. We are more likely to celebrate Passover with lamb burgers than a Seder plate. If you are part of Messianic communities, are Torah observant, or of another faith we hope that you still feel honored in how we present this information and find a new richness in how you understand scripture and connect with God.

Healing in the Hebrew Months: Part 1

As I mentioned before, my introduction to the Hebrew months came through Seneca's *Times and Seasons* box club. My background is in counseling and I now work as an inner healing practitioner so I couldn't help but notice the emotional themes to each month and the potential for healing when we lean into these rhythms.

One of the tools I use with my clients is tapping through body-meridian points while focusing on a specific issue or emotion. When I found out there were specific body parts associated with each month and that those body parts and correlating meridian points matched the emotional themes of the months, I knew I had to dig deeper to unlock the healing ripe in these seasons for my clients.

Here you'll gain a foundation of understanding the Hebrew calendar and the overall themes of each month. You'll see how the Hebrew months are mentioned throughout scripture and how they speak prophetically of Jesus our Messiah. As we look at the biblical significance of each month, we'll also highlight the emotional themes and give you a Captive Thought Therapy tapping exercise to use throughout the month.

Healing in the Hebrew Months: Part 2

Seneca had a dream where someone told her that every weed has a season in which it's vulnerable, and can easily be dealt with for good. The voice said not to waste time and effort on the wrong weeds for the season. Soon after that, a three-year research project unfolded which culminated in her *Times and*

Seasons subscription box club, and her contribution to our book set.

The explanations behind each Hebrew month, the original meaning of the corresponding constellations, the tribes that correlate to each, each tribe's stone, and the Gates of Jerusalem all come together to give us strategy throughout the year. Blessings, areas of healing, potential pitfalls and warfare are revealed when we align them all together.
When we follow the schedule God laid out in the stars, freedom in certain areas comes easier, and there are specific blessings to take advantage of. There are special things God wants to bring forth in our lives every month that will propel us forward into our destiny.

Healing in the Hebrew Months: Part 3
Del's book focuses on the connection between Hebrew letters, their gematria, musical frequencies, the A=432 concert pitch, and the blessings found within each letter. The letters demonstrate the

overall character of God and are meant to assist in our daily walk of intimacy with YHVH. As we learn to walk in that intimate place with Him, it brings healing to our being.

Del had an encounter where Jesus showed her "beyond the veil" in the tabernacle. In that experience, she watched the priest sing the names of God. As he did so, frequencies, in the form of color ribbons, floated around the Holy of Holies. Each sung musical note intermixed with a Name of God danced about the room interacting with the stones on the priest's breastplate along with all the items in and on the Ark of the Covenant.

Taking this experience as a cue to dig further into the mysteries of the Hebrew letters and musical frequencies, Del began a journey of discovery looking to see how this connection played out in musical language. Trained as a classical musician, Del's knowledge of music theory and history played a key role in her research that led down many rabbit trails before the answer revealed itself.

A Different Kind of Time

Two Different Calendars

Our Gregorian calendar has served us well with organizing time, but has disconnected us from the natural rhythms the rest of creation follows. The Hebrew calendar is a lunisolar calendar meaning that the months follow the moon but also account for the solar year and seasons. The days also start at sunset rather than sunrise.

"God called the light "day," and He called the darkness "night." Evening came and then morning: the first day." Genesis 1:5 (HCSB)

Because the lunar months are a few days shorter than our solar months, the Hebrew month start dates dance throughout our Gregorian months, moving back and forth between the same two months or so every few years. However because it is a lunisolar calendar rather than strictly lunar, every few years there is a leap month to keep the calendar aligned with the physical lunar seasons (spring, summer, fall, winter).

On the Gregorian solar calendar there is a leap day of February 29th every four years. On the lunisolar Hebrew calendar there is the leap month of a second Adar. The Hebrew leap years follow what is called a Metonic cycle, meaning that leap years occur seven times within a nineteen-year cycle. This works out to about every two-three years on years 3, 6, 8, 11, 14, 17, and 19. In 2022 we are in the eleventh year of the Metonic cycle.

The start of the year is also different with the Hebrew calendar. Much like we have our calendar year and school year that both mark different starting points, the Hebrew calendar has more than one New Year. While Rosh Hashanah in the month of Tishrei is considered the start of the civil year, the month of Nisan became the head of the ecclesiastical (spiritual) year for the Jewish people when Passover was established.

Lunar Concerns

One of the reasons many Christians have reluctance about paying any attention to the moon or lunar calendars is the way mythology, Wicca, and occultic practices attribute feminine deity to the moon and perform rituals in conjunction with the lunar cycle. While we certainly want to be careful about the meaning we attribute to the lunar calendar and the sources we are getting our information, it's silly to say the lunar calendar is off limits. Some ancient civilizations worshipped a sun god, but that hasn't stopped us from appreciating sunsets and sunrises or noting how certain colors at sunset can provide weather forecast information.

> *Then God said, "Let there be lights in the expanse of the heavens to separate the day from the night, and let them be for signs and for seasons and for days and years; and let them be for lights in the expanse of the heavens to give light on the earth"; and it was so.*
>
> *God made the two great lights, the greater light to govern the day, and the lesser light to govern the night; He made the stars also. God placed them in the expanse of the heavens to give light on the earth, and to govern the day and the night, and to separate the light from the darkness; and God saw that it was good.*
>
> Genesis 1:14-18 (NASB)

God gave us the sun and the moon to signify seasons and signs that He wants to communicate to us. Society has been pretty good about continuing to pay attention to the sun, but we've often neglected the moon and what it has to say about the glory God is revealing to us. The moon reflects the light of the sun as we are called to reflect the Light of the World.

The Biblical New Moon

Lunar events are described throughout scripture as being signs of God's moves. Israel knew the importance of the lunar calendar and set up feasts according to mark the new moons. Some historians argue that the observance of looking for the new moon was an act of worship; explaining that the ancient Israel definition of the "new moon" was actually the first sliver of a waxing crescent moon that is seen after what we consider a new moon when the moon is hidden by the earth's shadow.

Others say that the full moon is actually what Biblically is referred to as the new moon; and that our lack of connection to this method of counting time has left us disconnected from what God is trying to reveal to us through the luminaries.

Getting Back in Rhythm

Regardless of when the new moon technically occurs, what is clear is that we are missing out on the beautiful rhythm God set up with the lunar cycle. The switch from a lunisolar calendar to a strictly solar calendar stripped us of a sense of season.

When we pay attention to the lunar calendar, we are reconnected with the passage of time the way the world naturally experiences it. Our solar calendar makes it easier for modern society to be organized, but in our artificial organization we have lost touch with one of the ways God wants to communicate with us.

We forget how powerful the effects of the moon are, but go visit a beach and talk with local fishermen and they are intimately aware of the moon phases and how it affects the tides. Even far from shore we feel those shifts whether or not we are paying attention to them.

Engaging with the lunar cycle not only reconnects us to these natural rhythms but also reveals spiritual patterns we have already been following blindly. Our bodies have been aware of these patterns all along, but our minds never were taught.

Creation groans for us to understand our freedom as sons and daughters of God (Romans 8:18-24), yet we have not had ears to hear and eyes to see the things God has hidden for us to discover (Proverbs 25:2). As our eyes are opened to these patterns set into creation, we gain a fresh understanding of our authority and access to the depths of freedom and healing waiting to be claimed.

The Biblical Calendar

You will notice as you read scripture that not all of the months are referred to by name, or by a different name than we list here. For much of the Old Testament the months are mostly referred to by number. And then seemingly for no reason, in Nehemiah and Esther they begin to refer to the months by names and sometimes numbers as well.

The majority of these month names came from the time of Babylonian captivity and are Babylonian names the Jews adopted. The Babylonian calendar was very similar to the Hebrew calendar: it followed the lunar cycle, used the Metonic cycle, and its first month of the year was in the spring. It is likely Israel did not see it a major concession to use the Babylonian names when the rest of the calendar was very similar and they could still keep Sabbath, their fasts, and festivals. But why did they keep the Babylonian names for the months even after captivity? One explanation is a prophecy from Jeremiah:

> *Therefore behold, days are coming," declares the Lord, "when it will no longer be said, 'As the Lord lives, who brought up the sons of Israel out of the land of Egypt,' but, 'As the Lord lives, who brought up the sons of Israel from the land of the north and from all the countries where He had banished them.' For I will restore them to their own land which I gave to their fathers.*
>
> Jeremiah 16:14 (NASB)

Counting the months by number is a reference back to Egypt – it's the number of months since they were brought out of captivity. Calling the months by the Babylonian names is a reference to the Lord gathering his people back from Babylon and restoring them to the Promised Land.

Lost History

Christianity shifted in many ways with the Protestant Reformation due in large part to Martin Luther's Bible that made scripture accessible to the common man. One translation choice on Luther's part however led to the loss of historical understanding of the years between the Old and New Testaments. Luther's Bible was the first to separate out some books from the rest of scripture. He chose to place books that were not in the Masoretic Jewish text in a separate section between the Old and New Testaments. Ironically, these books which used to be commonly read, became hidden and forgotten by modern Protestants fitting with the name they are known by – apocrypha means hidden or secret.

Up until the late 1600s these apocryphal books were included in every King James Bible. In 1826 Bible societies decided to stop including the apocryphal books to save money on printing. Whether you believe these books to be equal standing with scripture or not, the historical accounts they contain provide crucial insight into the history between the end of Malachi and beginning of Matthew and the calendar the Jews followed.

Two books specifically give clarity to the religious world Jesus stepped into. 1 & 2 Maccabees give accounts of the Jewish history from 175BC to 134 BC. In 175 BC a new ruler in Syria, Antiochus Epiphanes, began oppressing the Jews, leading many to abandon their faith and follow pagan customs. By 169 BC Antiochus had plundered the temple and set up a fort nearby, installing traitorous Jews as the priests. Many Jews were killed, fell away from the faith, or hid in the mountains to survive while practicing their faith. In 167 BC on the 15th of Kislev, Antiochus desecrated the temple by setting up idols and offering sacrifices to pagan gods as prophesied by Daniel in Daniel 11:21-22; 29-32. All of the scrolls containing scripture were destroyed and the persecution intensified with the faithful being brutally killed.

Some of the Jews that hid became the Qumran community that maintained their own calendar. The dates of this calendar sometimes appear to be more accurate to scripture than the modern Jewish calendar followed today and the Qumran calendar bears similarity to the 364 day calendar found in the Dead Sea Scrolls of the book of Enoch.

The Maccabees Revolt that led to the events we celebrate at Hanukkah, also led to a reestablishment of the Hebrew calendar within the Jewish culture. As mentioned earlier in this chapter, the Hebrew calendar adopted Babylonian names during the exile. Along with the persecution under Antiochus, the time keeping rhythms of sabbaths, feasts, and fasts was also almost lost.

The Pharisees emerged shortly after the Maccabean revolt as a reaction to this loss of spiritual practice. So much had been lost or full of cultural mixture that the Pharisees were a movement focused on rightfully following the Torah. They were so careful to follow the letter of the law, that they created their own rules that were more restrictive to make certain they never violated the Torah. What started as a desire for faithful spiritual practice, became religious legalism as the Pharisees codified their extrabiblical rules into the Mishna. Many of Jesus' interactions with the Pharisees can be understood through this distinction between rabbinical rules in the Mishna and biblical law in the Torah.

In regards to the calendar, the modern Jewish calendar follows rules from the Mishna and oral tradition that are not in scripture for calculating dates. For example: Rosh Chodesh (the first of the month) does not fall with the new moon if the new moon falls on the sabbath; so looking strictly at scripture's Hebrew calendar will not always align with the modern counting of dates.

Where to Start Counting

What you will see throughout scripture is phrases like, "in the third month of the fourth year of the reign of king..." There are a few ways to interpret these references to time:

You could count that third month based on the actual date that king took the throne, or you could count it as the third month of the year in what was the fourth year of that king's reign. For example we might say, "in March of the fourth year of Washington's presidency."

In other places time is counted based on someone's life:

> *In the six hundredth year of Noah's life, on the seventeenth day of the second month--on that day all the springs of the great deep*

burst forth, and the floodgates of the heavens were opened.

Genesis 7:11 (NIV)

Again, it's unclear if this means in the second month after Noah's birthday, or the second month of the year when Noah was 600. For example my birthday is in July, so you could say in February when I was 30 or the second month after my 30th birthday which would have been September.

The other thing to consider with these mentions of months is where do you start counting? Tishrei is regarded as the seventh month but the beginning of the new year on the Hebrew civil calendar. But God established Nisan as the first month in Exodus 16.

First	Nisan	Tishrei
Second	Iyar	Cheshvan
Third	Sivan	Kislev
Fourth	Tammuz	Tevet
Fifth	Av	Shevat
Sixth	Elul	Adar
Seventh	Tishrei	Nisan
Eighth	Cheshvan	Iyar
Nineth	Kislev	Sivan
Tenth	Tevet	Tammuz
Eleventh	Shevat	Av
Twelfth	Adar	Elul

Noah was born before Exodus, so would the months have been counted from Tishrei then? Moses is regarded as the author of Genesis, so would he have counted from Nisan since he was there when God set that as the first month?

Historical books such as 1 & 2 Maccabees, Josephus, Jubilees, and Jasher as well as Rabbinical texts such as the Talmud, and Midrash often give us better clues to Biblical dates. From them it does seem that "second month" with Noah's story means Cheshvan and not Iyar, but other dates some of them reference seem to count from Nisan as month one so it still isn't clear.

Holidays and Harvests

To understand the calendar in scripture you also need to understand the schedule of feasts, fasts, and offerings as well as the agricultural rhythms. Dates are referenced more often by what holiday or harvest they were near than they are by calendar date or month.

Holidays and Harvests

Nisan	Passover Wave Offering	Barley harvest begins
Iyar	Second Passover	Barley Harvest finished
Sivan	Feast of Weeks/Shavuot, Pentecost	Wheat harvest begins
Tammuz	Shivah Asar B'Tammuz or Fast of Tammuz	Wheat harvest finished First figs
Av	Feast of New Wine	Grape harvest begins
Elul	Feast of New Oil, Wood Offering	Date harvest, Summer figs
Tishrei	Yom Teruah, Yom Kippur, Sukkot	Ploughing begins
Cheshvan		Ploughing finishes, Grain planting
Kislev	Beginning of Hanukkah	Grain planting
Tevet	End of Hanukkah *Asarah B'Tevet*	Rainy season
Shevat	Tu B'Shevat	Fruit trees bud
Adar	Fast of Esther, Purim	Flax harvest

Sorting it All Out

The more you dig into the calendar and scriptural time the more confusing and frustrating it can get; especially, since we likely don't have the exact calendar that Israel used back in Exodus. There are some that claim to have figured out the real Biblical calendar and decry any other calendars as heresy. And they could be right, but they too could also be wrong. It would be foolish to believe we know the exact calendar with certainty. Fortunately, the goal is not to pin down precise Biblical dates. The goal is to connect with God and allow Holy Spirit to speak to us through the calendar and spiritual rhythms.

My series co-authors and I have done our best to sort through the research out there, study scripture ourselves, and follow God's leading to give you the best idea we can of what goes with each month without having to dig into it yourself but we certainly do not claim perfection! Even scholars that have studied much longer than we have still disagree about the timing of certain biblical events,

Jesus' birth especially! So we won't be offended if you disagree, but we will encourage you to do your own research and not just quote what a single other source says without thinking through it yourself.

At the end of each month's chapter there is a list of other scripture references to the month. These references are compiled from multiple sources of information such as: verse mention of the date, agricultural calendar interpretation of the date, extrabiblical historical records, oral tradition, and logical calculation based on other events dated in scripture.

There are a few verses where only one extrabiblical source references the date; in those cases we have noted the source next to the reference. For the sake of readability we have chosen not to reference every source that was used to calculate a verse's month as most verses have three to four references each. We hope this seasonal glimpse of how biblical events occurred will deepen your engagement with scripture and enrich your relationship with God throughout the year.

The Hebrew Months

The months of the Hebrew year are: Nisan, Iyar, Sivan, Tammuz, Av, Elul, Tishrei, Chesvan, Kislev, Tevet, Shevat, and Adar. Each month holds unique spiritual significance and areas ripe for healing. Here is a quick overview of the focus for each month.

Nisan (Starts in March or April)

The month of Nisan is known as the month of miracles and redemption. It was the month when the Israelites were brought out of Egypt and is a season of stepping out of bondage and towards our promised lands.

Iyar (Starts in April or May)

The month of Iyar is known as the month of natural healing. The word Iyar, is actually a Hebrew acronym taken from Exodus 15:26, "*I Am the Lord your healer.*" It's also the verse where we get Jehovah Rapha, the Lord your healer, as a name of God.

Sivan (Starts in May or June)

The month of Sivan is known as the month of giving, alignment, and mercy. Sivan is when Moses received the Torah and 10 Commandments on Mt. Sinai. It's also when the disciples received the Holy Spirit during Pentecost.

Tammuz (Starts in June or July)

The month of Tammuz is known as the month of worship, vision, and covenant. Tammuz is when the Israelites made a golden calf to worship when they feared Moses would not return off Mt. Sinai. It is also when Caleb, Joshua, and the other ten spies searched out the Promised Land.

Av (Starts in July or August)

Av was destined to be the season of entering promised lands but instead became the low point in the Hebrew year. It's the month when the spies returned from the Promised Land giving a bad report, and Israel refused to enter into the blessing God had planned for them.

Elul (Starts in August or September)

Elul is the month that *the king is in the field.* Usually the king was in his castle where the common person could not just meet with him, but during this season he would set up a tent in the fields so that anyone could easily bring their concerns directly to him. It's a prophetic season pointing to the intimate access to God we now have through Christ's death and resurrection.

Tishrei (Starts in September or October)

Tishrei is the season of fall feasts with Yom Kippur and Rosh Hashanah. These High Holy Days are a season of completion, atonement, and harvest. It's a season of returning to God and embracing his glory.

Chesvan (Starts in October or November)

Chesvan is a season of new beginnings. It is the month that the flood began and also when Noah was able to leave the ark a year later. It is believed to be the season for the Messiah to come establish his temple.

Kislev (Starts in November or December)

Kislev is known as a season of security, trust, and bringing things full circle. It is the month that Hanukkah is celebrated marking the miracle of the oil lasting for the rededication of the temple. It is a season of lights, dreams, and success in battles from a place of peace.

Tevet (Starts in December or January)

Tevet is a month of authority. It's a season to prevail against our enemies, being angry but not sinning. It's a season of fasting and purification, reclaiming whatever the enemy has stolen from us.

Shevat (Starts in January or February)

Shevat is the month of New Year for Trees. It is a month of sowing righteousness and planning for blooms in generations to come. It's a season of building expectancy and faith for blessings to come.

Adar (Starts in February or March)

Adar means strength and is the month that Esther saved the Jewish from Haman's plot to kill them. It is a season of true identity. Esther was able to save her people when she revealed her true identity to the king. It's a month that depression and despair give way to hope and victory. It’s also the last month the Israelites spent in Egypt before crossing the Red Sea.

A Month by Any Other Spelling

You'll also notice that various sources spell certain months differently. This is because Biblical Hebrew contains no vowels and there are multiple ways you could choose to write a Hebrew word with English letters (transliteration). For example you may see Tammuz written with two m's or one – Tamuz, or Nisan written with one or two s's. All of the spellings are considered correct and it's a matter of preference which spelling you use.

The Twelve Tribes and the Twelve Months

If you're familiar with other teachings on the Hebrew months you may notice that we order the tribes differently than some. Seneca goes into detail about this in her book, but the basic reason why is there not a "correct" way to order them. At various times scripture lists the tribes by birth, by blessing, by marching order, and by their camp arrangement.

Most people that talk about the months and tribes haven't really given thought to this and are just following the marching order because that's what they have seen others do, and those others were likely following the order in Sefer Yetzirah (a Jewish text that predates the Kabbalah).

You can read more of Seneca's explanation of all this here:
www.healinginthehebrewmonths.com/how-the-12-tribes-are-associated-with-the-12-months

Some Resources for Keeping up with Hebrew Months

Chronological Study Bible

Aside from the Hebrew months, the chronology of scripture can be confusing with how the books are traditionally ordered. A chronological study Bible can help you get a sense of time and what passages are describing the same event – like how Jeremiah's prophecies fit with the historical accounts of Chronicles. Just search "Chronological Study Bible" online and you'll find several options.

Sign up for Email Reminders

Give us your email address at
www.healinginthehebrewmonths.com
and we'll send you a free email reminder when each new month starts.

Get a Hebrew Calendar

There are several great options out there for Jewish calendars. We recommend the Healing in the Hebrew Months calendar that goes along with the book series. It includes a summary of the significant things each month, Hebrew dates, and holidays all on a standard Gregorian calendar. Get yours here:

www.healinginthehebrewmonths.com/store

Add the Dates to Your Phone

Both iPhone and Android have options that will let you add the Hebrew dates to your phone's calendar. On iPhone go to Settings > Calendar > Alternate Calendars and select Hebrew. It will show the dates on your calendar app as well as the lock screen.

For Android the options are not as straight-forward but there are several apps available with the Hebrew calendar or you can add it in settings in Google Calendar.

Your Hebrew Birthday

Another fun thing you can do with the calendar is lookup your birthday according to the Hebrew dates. Because the Hebrew calendar shifts through the Gregorian calendar, your birthday according to each system will rarely coincide. We fully support celebrating both dates for double the presents and cake. Look up your Hebrew birthday here:

www.healinginthehebrewmonths.com/your-hebrew-birthday

Healing in Community

If you want to connect with others following the Hebrew months, The *Healing in the Hebrew Months* Facebook group is where you can find community with like-minded Christians that are also pursuing the healing ripe in each Hebrew month.

www.facebook.com/groups/HealingintheHebrewMonths

Charts and Posters

On our website you'll also find charts and posters to keep the months' symbols handy. The master chart on the next page pulls all the information from all three books together in one place and is also available as a pdf download on our site:

www.healinginthehebrewmonths.com/store

Healing in the Hebrew Months Master Chart

Month	Nisan	Iyar	Sivan	Tammuz	Av	Elul	Tishrei	Cheshvan	Kislev	Tevet	Shevat	Adar
Meaning	To move or start, miracles	I am God, your healer	Season or time	Unknown, Babylonian Deity	Father	I am my beloved's; my beloved is mine	Head of the Year	Eighth month	Trust, hope	Good	Unknown	Strength
Blessing	Redemption & freedom	Disease prevention	Covenant	Practical revelation	Sonship, Father's promises	God's presence	Promotion	Rest and transition	Sleep and dreams	Seeing what we couldn't before	Imperceptible shifts for new fruit	Joy
Tribe	Gad	Asher	Benjamin	Zebulon	Judah	Naphtali	Levi	Dan	Joseph	Simeon	Rueben	Issachar
Gem	Gray Agate	Olivine/Peridot	Rainbow Jasper	Quartz	Chalcedony	Amethyst	Sardonyx	Turquoise	Black Onyx	Chrysoprase	Carnelian	Lapis
Constellation	Aries	Taurus	Gemini	Cancer	Leo	Virgo	Libra	Scorpio	Sagittarius	Capricorn	Aquarius	Pisces
Decans	Cassiopeia, Cetus, Perseus	Orion, Eridanus, Auriga	Lepus, Canis Major, Canis Minor	Ursa Major, Ursa Minor, Argo	Hydra, Crater, Corvus	Coma, Centaurus, Bootes	Crux, Lupus, Corona	Serpens, Ophichus, Hercules	Lyra, Ara, Draco	Saggita, Aquilla, Delphinus	Southern Fish, Pegasus, Cygnus	The Band, Cepheus, Andromeda
Gate	Sheep	Fish	Old	Valley	Dung	Fountain	Water	Horse	East	Miphkad	Epharim	Prison
Letter	Heh ה	Vav ו	Zayin ז	Chet ח	Tet ט	Yod י	Lamed ל	Nun נ	Samech ס	Ayin ע	Tsadi ת	Qoph ק
Musical Note	E	G	B-flat	C	A	C	B	A-flat	B	D	F-sharp	A-flat
Emotion	Hope	Redemption	Generosity	Adoration	Discernment	Intimacy	Security	Revelation	Dreaming	Authority	Righteousness	Joy
Body Part	Right Foot	Right Kidney	Left Foot	Right Hand	Left Kidney	Left Hand	Reproductive Organs	Intestines	Stomach	Liver	Throat	Spleen
Holidays	Passover, Wave Offering	2nd Passover	Shavout, Pentecost	Fast of Tammuz	Tish'a B'Av, Feast of New Wine	Feast of New Oil, Wood Offering	Yom Teruah/Rosh Hoshannah, Yom Kippur, Sukkot	None	Hanukkah begins	Hanukkah ends, Fast of Tevet	Tu B'Shevat/New Year for Trees	Fast of Esther, Purim
Area of Healing	Enslavement	Bitterness & Unforgiveness	Double-mindedness, internal conflict	Negativity & fear	Father wounds, self-worth	Rejection, isolation, spiritual vision	Performance mentality	Moving into new identity	Trust issues with God	Anger, victimization, judgment	Letting go of unproductive areas	Identity
Warfare	Declare blessings over negative situations	Guard against distractions or being rattled by temporary circumstances	Bind fear of deep spiritual experiences	Be vigilant against idolatry	Guard against listening to bad counsel	Don't jump through religious hoops	Don't get caught up focusing on sin	Fight against obstacles to your call	Battle from a place of rest	Bind influencing that color your perception with anger	Fight fear of change, complacency	Enemy reaps what he sows, use laughter as a weapon

All information taken from the *Healing in the Hebrew Months* book series. See the books for more information. www.HealingintheHebrewMonths.com

Tapping into the Month

Each month has a Captive Thought Therapy (CTT) tapping exercise to help you go deeper with the emotional theme of the month. Feel free to skip these if you are just interested in the month information.

CTT is the method I use with my clients and is a Christian approach to healing that combines tapping with inner healing prayer to help you take your thoughts captive and find greater breakthroughs in emotional and spiritual health.

Where Captive Thought Therapy differs from other tapping protocols you may be familiar with is the three different rounds of tapping and the inner healing tools we use throughout each round. Unlike other tapping we also spend time asking God to fill us up with the good and declaring his truth over ourselves, instead of just focusing on clearing out the negative emotion. All of CTT is partnered with Holy Spirit through prayer to not only release the negative emotions and lies but also fill up with God's truth and heavenly perspective.

Meridian Lines

Tapping therapies like CTT work by engaging the meridian line system of the body through acupressure (the tapping) while focusing on the emotional content causing distress. When we experience trauma, our bodies store an energetic signature of the emotions we feel within the meridian system, much like how a computer stores information as electric signatures on a hard drive. When these blockages are not dealt with, we have disproportionate emotional reactions to triggering experiences. The “file” on anger gets triggered and instead of just the anger appropriate to the situation, all the anger we’ve stored up comes out as well.

Meridian lines are the system of pathways in the body by which these energetic signatures flow and are stored. Energy meaning: electrical, physical, scientific energy – not mystical energy as some in the New Age movement describe it. They are the same system used in acupuncture, chiropractic, and Traditional Chinese Medicine (TCM) to alleviate physical and emotional symptoms. Acupuncture works with meridian lines by placing pins as little antennas to draw the flow of energy around any blockages in the meridian lines. Chiropractic uses physical manipulations to put the body back into alignment wherever the improper flow in the meridian lines has pushed the body out of alignment.

However, the problem acupuncturists and chiropractors both run into, is that their adjustments do not always stick. The emotional blocks in the meridian lines have not been dealt with directly, just the physical symptoms of the meridian lines being blocked have been addressed; so we continue to have the same symptoms over and over, needing repeated physical adjustments or feeling stuck in our emotional responses. This is where methods such as tapping have made huge strides in dealing with the emotional blockages – complementing the work of chiropractic, acupuncture, and counseling. Tapping in general addresses these emotional blocks and with CTT we take it even deeper by praying through the emotions and dealing with the spiritual aspects as well.

Quantum Marvels

So how is tapping different than just acupressure? At the quantum level everything has weight – our thoughts, our emotions, the physical things we think of as having weight, all of it. The convenient thing about this weight is that God designed positive, happy, heavenly minded things to weigh more than negative, sad, sin and death things. If you drop a bowling ball into a swimming pool it makes a big splash because the bowling ball weighs more than the water; it displaces the water out of the pool. The same is true with our thoughts and emotions; positive thoughts that weigh more at the quantum level displace negative thoughts. This is why we don't just focus on clearing out the negative emotion, we also take time to fill up on the positive and truth from scripture.

The observer effect is another quantum principle that applies to tapping. At the macro-physics level we can know where something is, how fast it is moving, and where it will end up, calculating trajectory. At the quantum level we are not able to calculate trajectory, because as soon as the object is observed those variables shift. When we focus our attention on our emotions it has a similar effect, shifting how those emotions have been stuck.

The good news is you don't have to be a quantum physicist to benefit from these principles, but it is amazing how intricately God designed our bodies to work and that he wired us for health and healing! If you do want to delve more into quantum theory I recommend Quantum Glory by Phil Mason and The Physics of Heaven by Judy Franklin and Ellyn Davis.

Psychological Reversal

Much of our emotional distress is caused by psychological reversals – a fancy way of saying lies we are believing about God, ourselves, other people, or how the world works. In other tapping models the side of hand point at the end of every exercise is known as the psychological reversal point. In addition to breaking off lies with the collarbone statements, we end each round of tapping with this side of hand point as another way to engage the body in aligning with God's truth.

While the tapping helps move stuck emotions along, correcting these reversals through forgiveness and rejecting lies is often the most powerful part of the process. Whether or not you tap consistently, the single best thing you can do for growing in health is staying intimately connected to God and the truth that comes from him.

Power of Three

Part of what makes CTT different than other tapping is the three different rounds we go through in each exercise. Neurobiologically our brains need repetition to really take notice of a concept and form new pathways, three times seems to be the point where we really begin to remember a new idea. Practically, three is a strong cord that we can easily remember and repeat. Ecclesiastes 4:12 (HCSB) "And if someone overpowers one person, two can resist him. A cord of three strands is not easily broken."

Spiritually, each round represents body-mind-spirit and the needs of each in processing emotion. "Then God said, "Let Us make man in Our image, according to Our likeness." Genesis 1:26 (HCSB, emphasis mine)

We know that God is a triune being – Father God, Jesus, and Holy Spirit. So when he said, "let Us make man in Our image," that includes the triune nature of God. Tripartite means consisting of three parts body-mind-spirit.

Body

Our physical beings with senses of sight, smell, touch, sound, and taste. Jesus is our picture of the body. He came in physical form, lived as a human, felt what we felt, died physically for our salvation, and was resurrected physically for our restoration.

Mind

Our mind, will, and emotions comprise the soul – the home of our imaginations, creativity, memories, thoughts, and affections. Some even refer to this aspect of our being as the tripartite soul because of these three components. Father God is our picture of the mind, will, and emotions. Scripture is full of emotional language, sharing his thoughts with us, his feelings, and his desire for his people.

Spirit

Our personal spirit that communes with God, experiences the fruits of The Spirit, receives conviction, and engages in prayer, worship, and fellowship. We are filled with Holy Spirit but we also have our personal spirit. Holy Spirit is our perfect example that our personal spirits connect with.

Body Part of the Month

Now why does any of this matter for the Hebrew months? Each meridian line has an organ system associated with it and peak times throughout the day that those systems are active (the chart on the next page shows when). We'll look each month at the body part traditionally associated with the month and how the corresponding meridian can give us clues to the emotions we need to process with God. Even if you don't use the CTT tapping exercises, at least take a moment to pray over the month's body part and ask God if there is anything he wants to show you about that body part or potentially related emotions.

Body Meridian Clock of Emotions

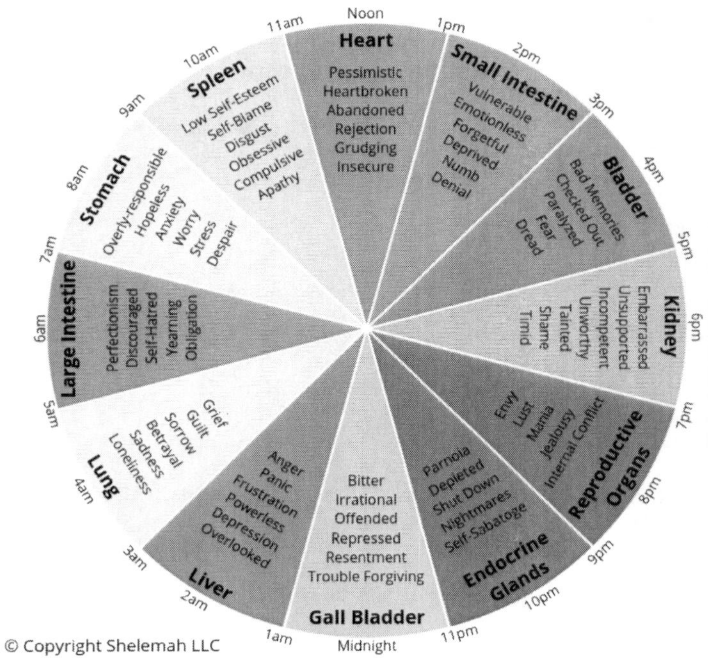

How to use the Tapping Exercises

Unlocking the Code

Each month's tapping exercise has a coded line telling you which points to tap and a diagram showing where the points are located. Look over the points first so you know where to tap. Use your finger tips to tap lightly 3-5 times on each point as you go through the exercise. You'll use the same tapping pattern for each of the three rounds of the exercise.

If the points have two locations as with the collarbones (CB) or under the arms (A), it is fine to just tap on one side of the points. If there are any mobility or other health issues that would prevent you from tapping on the points you can also hold each point pressing lightly instead of tapping, or have someone else tap the points on your body for you as you engage with the rest of the exercise.

Keep Tapping as You Move Your Eyes

The BH(30)+B on each exercise means the BH (Back of Hand) point, for 30 seconds, while also engaging bi-lateral brain stimulation. If you are working with a CTT coach or practitioner, they will move their fingers back and forth for you to follow with your eyes and will keep time for the thirty seconds.

If you're working alone, you can tap your feet back and forth, walk around, or look back and forth between the corners of a room. Or if you're familiar with EMDR music, you can use headphones with those specially panned tracks.

When you do the exercises on your own, it is easier to keep an internal sense of when about thirty seconds has passed instead of trying to count to thirty as you also tap and focus on the exercise for that round. If you end up going longer than thirty seconds that is fine. The goal is to engage both sides of the brain back and forth, through movements that cross the vertical hemisphere of the body, for at least 30 seconds.

Deep Breath In, Let it Out Slowly

Before you begin tapping through each round, take a nice deep breath in through your nose and let it out slowly through your mouth to settle yourself and prepare for the exercise.

You can keep your eyes open or closed as you tap, whatever feels most comfortable. Some find it helpful to speak out loud what they are tapping through, repeating the emotion, praying, or repeating the verse from round three. Whatever helps you stay present with the emotion you are tapping through is fine to do.

What Comes to Mind?

Tapping is not like meditation. Instead of emptying our minds and focusing on one thing, we are actively inviting God to bring to mind what's related, where the emotion started, how he sees what we're going through. If your grocery list comes to mind, push that thought aside, but if a random memory from childhood, another experience, or a person comes to mind, let those thoughts come and ask God what he wants to show you about how they related to the emotion. Then use the Forgiveness Tapping or Collarbone Statements to process what came up as you tapped through the round.

Round 1

The first round through an exercise you focus on the negative you want to release. Before you begin tapping, check in with yourself on how strongly you feel that negative emotion on a scale of 1–10 with 10 being the strongest. You do not have to currently feel the emotion, or try to make yourself feel it. When you think about what it feels like to experience the emotion, how strong does it feel?

How easily can you get in touch with that feeling? Once you have your number, make note of it and tap through the exercise.

When you finish tapping, check in with yourself again and see where the number is. You want to see this number come down by at least one before moving onto the second round. If the number doesn't go down, goes down only a little, or jumps up, check if there is any Forgiveness Tapping you need to do. Someone may have come to mind as you tapped or you may have been aware of someone you need to forgive for this emotion before you even started tapping. You can also pray and ask God if there is anyone you need to forgive, taking a minute to listen.

If you do any Forgiveness Tapping check in again with the number. If it still has not come down, check again if there is anyone else you need to forgive or repeat round one of the exercise.

Especially when you first start tapping you may need to repeat a round just because you were struggling to focus on the emotion – the dog barked and distracted you, trying to tap and focus felt like learning to walk and chew gum, that grocery list kept demanding your attention, etc.

Round 2

The second round through the exercise you are going to focus on the positive opposite emotion you want to increase. You can imagine what that positive emotion would feel like, invite God to fill you up with that positive emotion, ask God to show you what he wants to give you instead of that negative emotion, or ask God to give you his perspective on it.

Keep in mind the number you got at the end of round one and check in with the number again after tapping through round two. Don't get a new number for the positive emotion, stick with tracking the number you got for the negative emotion at the beginning of the exercise. If the number has not gone down, has stayed the same, or has jumped back up after round two, use the Collarbone Statements to affirm the truth you need with this emotion. By the end of round two we ideally want to see the number at a six or lower.

If you use Collarbone Statements, check in again with the number. If it still has not come down, check again if there are any additional Collarbone Statements you need to do or repeat round two of the exercise.

Round 3

The third round through the exercise, we want to seal everything up with truth. Each exercise has a suggested verse that relates to the emotion. Feel free to substitute other verses as God highlights the truth you need to remember most. I love using Biblegateway.com to look at multiple translations of a verse, and often will end up using my own paraphrase of a few translations combined when I tap. Another great resource for finding other verses is www.openbible.info/topics/ it combines a general search engine with a Bible search to give you relevant verses that may not have the exact search word in them.

As you tap through the third time, you'll repeat the verse over and over, either out loud or in your head. If the verse is too long to easily repeat, read through it first and pick a reminder statement you can repeat as you tap. For example:

> *May the God of hope fill you with all joy and peace as you trust in him, so that you may overflow with hope by the power of the Holy Spirit.*
>
> Romans 15:13 (NIV)

That's a bit long to repeat the whole verse, but you could use "God of hope fill me" or "As I trust in him" as reminder statements.

After tapping through round three, check in again with that number you've been tracking for the emotion. Ideally you want to get it below a three by the end of this third round of tapping. If the number is still above a three or has gone up instead of down after this round of tapping, ask God if there is any more Forgiveness Tapping or Collarbone Statements you need to do. You can also repeat the third round of tapping and check the number again.

Daily or As Needed

Use the tapping exercises daily or in moment as you find yourself dealing with the emotion. You may not have time to go through all three rounds each day getting the emotion to a three or less, but going through all three rounds is still helpful to clear out the negative, fill up with the positive, and seal it all up with truth.

If you are in a situation when you cannot use the tapping exercises, just tapping the collarbones or back of hand point can be very grounding and help you get through a heightened emotional state.

Layer by Layer

Every time you tap, you're removing a layer of that emotional trigger. Don't get discouraged if you have to work on the same emotion for a while. God can heal in the instantly, but he also walks with us through the healing process. It took years for all those layers to build up; it will take time to clear them off. You might keep seeing the same things come up over and over as you work through the exercises, but you are not just going in circles, you are climbing a spiral staircase! With each step you're getting a new perspective on that view and making forward progress

Tapping Videos

Tapping makes a lot more sense when you see it done instead of just reading about it. Each month has a free video showing you how to do the exercise.

You can find all the videos here:
URL and Password are both case sensitive
Videos: http://bit.ly/HebrewMonthsTapping
Password: RipeInEachSeason

Tapping Points

TH Top of Head
EB Eye Brow
T Temples
E Under Eyes
UN Under Nose
CH Chin
CB Collar Bone
SS Sore Spot
A Under Arms
R Bottom of Ribcage

TB Thumb
IF Index Finger
MF Middle Finger
PF Pinkie Finger
BH Back of Hand
SH Side of Hand

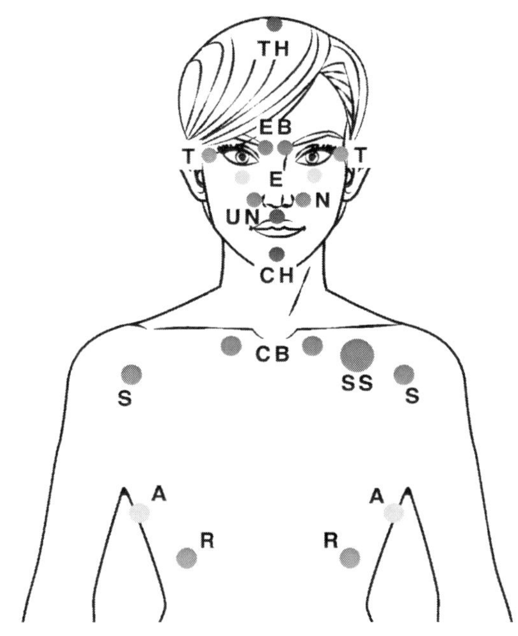
TH
EB
T
T
E
N
UN
CH
CB
SS
S
S
A
A
R
R

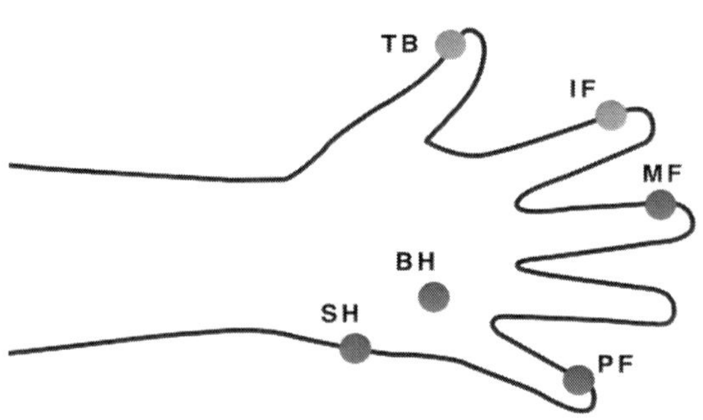
TB
IF
MF
BH
SH
PF

Forgiveness & Truth

Deal with What Comes Up

As you go through the tapping exercise you will likely uncover places of forgiveness that are needed or lies that you've believed that you need to reject. Tapping isn't like meditation. The goal isn't to empty our minds, but to let Holy Spirit speak into our emotions, bring peace where there was chaos, and heal the places that are hurting.

If you find yourself thinking about things that feel disconnected from the emotion, ask Holy Spirit about it, he's likely trying to show you something.

You can also use the Forgiveness Tapping and Collar Bone Statements for agreeing with truth described below to address what Holy Spirit highlights as you tap through the emotion.

You Can Hear

Throughout the process, invite Holy Spirit to show you what he has to say about the emotions, forgiveness, and the truths you need to displace lies. You can hear Holy Spirit. Don't let fears about your thoughts getting in the way or him being silent keep you from listening.

Often the first thought you have after asking him to speak is what he's trying to tell you. You may hear him more as a feeling, picture, or impression than full sentence conversation; but when you come with expectancy that he is speaking you'll be amazed how well you can hear him.

Many times, just rejecting the lie that he doesn't speak to you or has nothing to say is all it takes to open up your hearing.

Get Help When You Need It

If you get stuck and feel it would be helpful to have someone walk through the process with you, I recommend working with a Captive Thought Therapy practitioner or a counselor trained in EFT. You can find CTT practitioners at www.CaptiveThoughtTherapy.com

Forgiveness

With each emotion you may find there are people you need to forgive. Use forgiveness statements by themselves or with the tapping exercises to help forgiveness sink deep into body–mind–spirit.

Forgiveness is not the same as reconciliation. You do not have to be in relationship with that person again to forgive them. Reconciliation requires both parties to participate. Forgiveness just requires you. By forgiving you release yourself from the offenses you've been holding and the self–made prison they've kept you in.

You also do not have to feel like forgiving. With the forgiveness statements you are declaring your desire to forgive. You may have to continue to choose to forgive several times before you really feel it.

But I've Already Forgiven Them

Frequently I'll have a client say, "Oh, I've already forgiven them," when forgiving a certain person comes up in session. Sometimes this is a resistance to really forgiving — trying to avoid dealing with their feelings towards that person. But often it comes from a genuine place of having already done a lot of forgiveness work in regards to that person and feeling like it dishonors the work they've already done to forgive that person again.

What we fail to realize about forgiveness is that we are forgiving an offense not just a person. You may have already forgiven your dad for a lot of things, but there still may be some offenses that need forgiving.

No matter how thoroughly you've forgiven him for those other things, the offenses left unforgiven will hurt you and the relationship.

People that have deeply hurt us will likely need to be forgiven multiple times and for multiple things. Not because we didn't do a good job of forgiving them the first time, but because forgiveness is a process and a continual choice to release the offenses.

The legal system is a helpful way to think about forgiveness and offenses. The courts don't charge a person and find them guilty or not guilty in general. They charge a person with a specific offense or list of offenses. When we forgive it is the same way. We are releasing each individual offense over to a higher court – where God is judge and jury instead of us.

Will I Ever be Done Forgiving?

When there's someone you've had to forgive a lot you may wonder when you'll ever be done forgiving them. The need to continually forgive someone may never end, but your experience of needing to forgive them will change over time. Peter asked Jesus in Matthew 18:21-22 how many times he must forgive someone, and Jesus' response was, "Seventy times seven." Meaning, that we must forgive repeatedly, as many times as it takes.

There will be many offenses we need to forgive for people that we have spent a lot of time with or who have hurt us in very violating ways. Much like soul ties, time + vulnerability is a recipe for lots hurts that need to be forgiven.

If you find yourself asking, "do I really have to forgive them again?" It's a good sign there are still more offenses that need releasing. When you truly are living with a heart of forgiveness towards someone you won't have to wonder if you need to forgive them again; any inkling of offense will be met with a swift desire to forgive rather than questioning if forgiveness is necessary.

What Can You Forgive them For?

Often when a client has been deeply hurt and is unwilling to forgive, I'll ask if there is anything they can forgive that person for. It may take a few minutes of thought and prayer, but they usually can think of something small to forgive, which opens up a heart of forgiveness towards that person.

If you're struggling to forgive someone it may help to start with effects of the offense before forgiving the actual offenses. For example: start with forgiving for how they made you feel afraid, or forgiving for how their actions taught you lies about the world, before forgiving them for the action that hurt you.

Perceived is Believed

Offenses are about the resentments we've held in our own hearts –the ways we've felt hurt. You may need to forgive someone for an offense they didn't actually commit, but because you perceived it that way you need to release the resentment. The judgements we make against others and the resentments we hold are not always based in truth. If your mom didn't let you have cookies right before bed as a child you may have resented her for being mean. When you forgive your mom for being mean, you aren't saying that she actually was mean, you're acknowledging that in your heart you had judged her as mean and need to let go of that judgement.

Matthew 7:2 reminds us that, "For in the way you judge, you will be judged; and by your standard of measure, it will be measured to you" (NASB). Often forgiveness is all that is needed to release a judgment. But you can also follow up with some Collarbone Statements repenting for making the judgment, and affirming the truth about that situation.

Forgiving God

Since forgiveness is needed even for perceived offenses, we sometimes need to forgive God as well, although he is holy and has done nothing wrong. In our woundedness we believe lies about who God is and his heart towards us, and through these lies we hold offense towards him.

It may sound strange to say something like, "I forgive God for not protecting me." But if in your heart you believe the lie that he didn't protect you, it doesn't help to piously cling to the truth that he always protects us when the offense you're holding onto says otherwise.

Pretending the offense isn't there doesn't help you heal. It's worth the risk of sounding unorthodox to be honest about the offenses you need to forgive. God already knows your heart, he knows the offense and resentment you hold towards him, and he's just waiting for you to forgive him so there's nothing between you anymore.

Forgiveness Tapping

When you forgive you'll repeat a short forgiveness statement three times as you tap on your fingertips.

Tie the forgiveness statement to the emotion being cleared and keep them short and repeatable since you'll be saying the statement three times. For example, "I forgive this person for making me feel this emotion."

If you can't think of a specific person you need to forgive but feel that forgiveness is needed, you can forgive more generally, "I forgive anyone who has made me feel this emotion." Sometimes starting with a general forgiveness statement will bring to mind specific people you also need to forgive and then you can just repeat the forgiveness tapping with a new forgiveness statement.

You may notice that as you repeat the forgiveness statement you feel tongue-tied or go blank on what the statement was by the third time repeating it. This is actually a good sign that something is shifting as the emotion lifts and you begin to feel the forgiveness release.

Forgiving Yourself

As you forgive yourself, tap continually on the side of your index finger at the nail and repeat the forgiveness statement three times. Then tap on the side of your hand three to five times.

Forgiving Others

If you are forgiving another person, tap continually on the side of your pinky finger at the nail. Repeat the forgiveness statement three times, and then tap on the side of your hand.

Forgiving God

When forgiving God, tap continually on the side of your middle finger while repeating the forgiveness statement three times. When you're done, tap the side of your hand three to five times. This tapping point could also be used for "God forgives me" forgiveness statements.

Sample Forgiveness Statements

- I forgive myself for letting fear control me
- I forgive my mom for teaching me fear was normal
- I forgive anyone who has made me feel rejected
- I forgive God for not protecting me
- I forgive God for allowing this situation to continue
- God forgives me for trusting this emotion over him

Forgiveness Tapping Points

IF Index Finger: Forgiving Yourself
MF Middle Finger: Forgiving God
PF Pinkie Finger: Forgiving Others
SH Side of Hand: Tap at end of forgiving

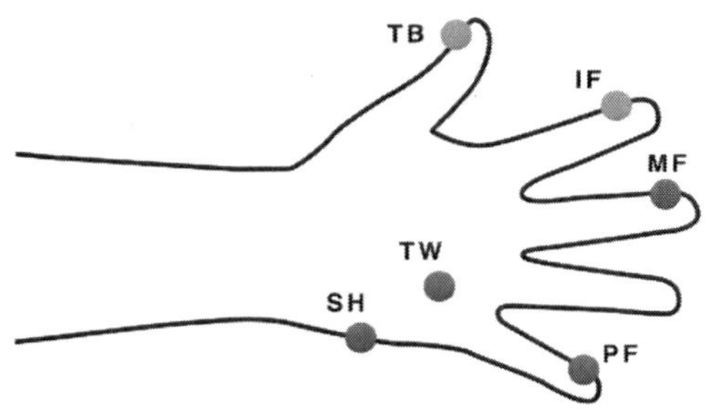

Agreeing with the Truth

Collarbone statements are a great way to get your head and heart to agree on the truth. As you go through the tapping exercises you may find places where you are struggling to believe the truth or you may identify a lie that was believed with the emotion you were clearing. You may also identify things you need to repent for such as: sinning against others in how you express an emotion, or going outside of God's plan for meeting your needs to meet them in your own power. You may also need to break agreement with an emotion as part of the repentance process.

With collarbone statements we are not naming and claiming something we want to be true, we are affirming God's truth despite our circumstances. Reality might be that you are in a painful relationship or situation, we don't deny reality, but we affirm God's truth which is higher than our present reality – "Even if this situation doesn't change, I can be filled with God's peace." Sometimes those realities carry unprocessed grief we need to mourn and allow God in to comfort us.

Whatever Collarbone Statement you need, tap or rub your collarbone points as you repeat the statement three times, then tap on the side of hand point when you are done.

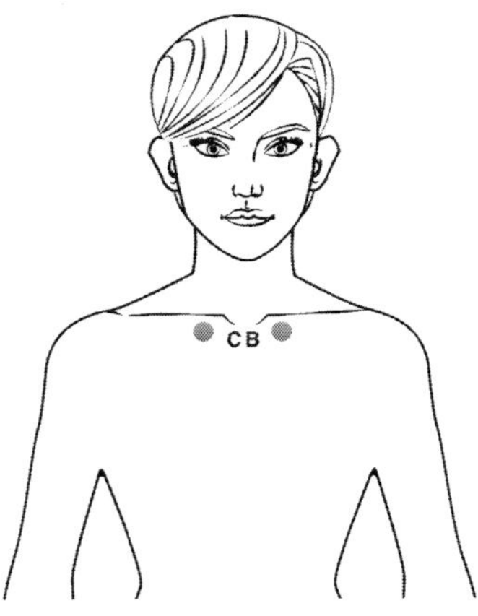

You may not feel a shift in connecting with that truth right away, and that's okay. You can repeat the Collarbone Statements as needed. You may also find that after you do one Collarbone Statement, others you need come to mind. Invite Holy Spirit into the process and let him guide you into all truth.

Sample Collarbone Statements

- Even though I'm scared, I can trust God to protect me.
- I am fearfully and wonderfully made.
- I am safe to process these emotions.
- Fear is a liar, and I don't have to listen to it.
- I can be fully me and fully accepted.
- Even though I feel this emotion now, I don't have to feel it forever.
- I reject the lie that _____, and accept the truth that ______.
- I break agreement with this emotion, and repent for trusting it to protect me instead of God.
- I acknowledge this loss, and invite God to comfort me.

Scriptures also make for great collarbone statements. Be sure to not just repeat verses, but make them personal, switching out "you" language for "I" and "me" language.

Nisan ניסן

Starts in March or April

The month of Nisan is known as the month of miracles and redemption. It became the head of the year for the Jewish people when Passover was established (Exodus 12). So, if you're wondering why we are starting in the Spring when you've heard of the Jewish new year being Rosh Hashanah in the Fall, that's why! Much like we have our calendar year and school year that both mark different starting points, the Hebrew calendar has more than one "new year".

In Exodus 16 Nisan is referred to as Aviv, which was an agricultural term referring to the growth stage of barley in the spring. In modern Hebrew the word just means spring. During the Babylonian captivity the month began to be referred to as Nisan and that name has since stuck (Nehemiah 2:1; Esther 3:7).

Nisan is associated with speech. What we say to ourselves and about ourselves is so powerful. Pivotal moments in Nehemiah and Esther's stories hinged on them being brave with their voices. And Moses used his voice for God to demand Pharaoh, "Let my people go!" (Exodus 5:1)

While we clear out the negative emotions, it's even more important to spend time speaking truth over yourself. You can speak truth along with this month's tapping algorithm, but you can also use the collarbone exercises to engage the body as you meditate on truth.

Each month also has a part of the body or an organ system that is typically associated with it. This is significant because emotions tend to be stored in certain parts of the body. The tapping exercises for each month include points connected to these body systems. For Nisan the body part is the right foot. The liver and stomach meridian lines run through the foot and some emotions commonly associated with those organs are hopelessness, anxiety, low self-esteem, frustration, anger, and depression.

The meridians also have times of day that they are more active. For the liver 1-3 a.m. and stomach 7-9 a.m. are times to pay attention. If you notice your sleep being disturbed or feeling more emotional at these times it's a good sign that there's some emotional stuff that needs to be released.

The emotion we are focusing on this month is hope. Nisan was the season when the Israelites where brought out of Egypt. It's a season of stepping out of bondage and towards our promised lands. But to take those steps we need to leave behind any hopelessness that has held us back. It's hard to believe in miracles and promised lands to come if you don't have hope.

Even though Israel set out for their promised land in Nisan they struggled with hope and trusting God along their journey, and it wasn't until Nisan several decades later that they crossed the Jordan into the promised land (Joshua 4:19; 1 Chronicles 12:15).

Scripture does tell us that, "*hope deferred makes the heart sick*", but it also goes on to say that, "*desire fulfilled is a tree of life.*" Proverbs 13:12 (ESV) As you go through the tapping exercises this month take time to grieve those hopes deferred. It's ok to be honest about our disappointments and hurts, but don't just stop at grieving. Allow yourself to dream again, to hope again.

"*Any area of my life for which I have no hope is under the influence of a lie.*"

-Bill Johnson

As you go through this month pay attention to the areas where you struggle to have hope. When you identify an area, ask Jesus what lies you are believing and what the truth is. Then declare, "I reject the lie that ___." and do the Collarbone Statements explained on page 42 with the truth you identify.

I'm praying for you this month that God would fill your sleep with dreams of new hope and desires fulfilled. As we spend the next year journeying towards our Promised Land, we're going to need the hope we cultivate this month.

Other Scripture References to Nisan

Genesis 8:4

Genesis 12; 35:1-15; 37:12-35 (According to Jubilees)

Exodus 13:4; 40

Leviticus 23:5

Numbers 9; 20:1; 28:16; 33:3

Joshua 5

2 Kings 23

1 Chronicles 27

2 Chronicles 29:3,17; 29:17; 35

Ezra 6:19; 7-8; 10:17

Esther 3:7, 12

Ruth 2

Song of Solomon 6:11

Ezekiel 29:17-21; 30:20; 45

Daniel 10

Matthew 21; 26; 27; 28

Mark 11; 14; 16

Luke 2:41-51; 19; 20; 22; 24

John 2:13-25; 5:1-6; 6; 11-20

Acts 12

Nisan Tapping

CTT Exercise for Hope:

E – A – R – UN – BH+B(30) – SH

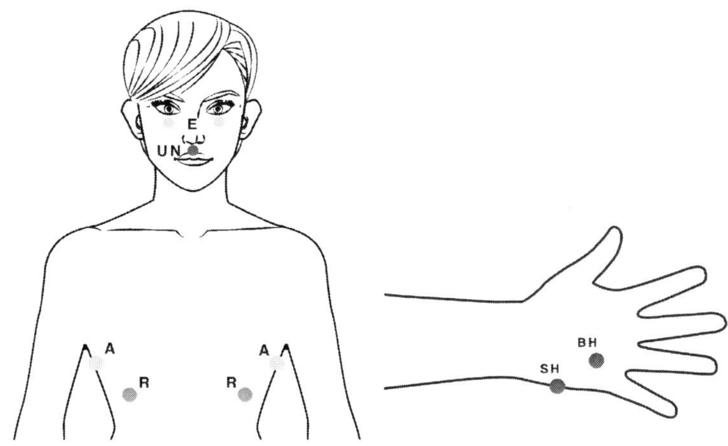

Tapping Points

E	Under Eyes
A	Under Arms
R	Bottom of Rib Cage
UN	Under Nose
BH	Back of Hand
B	Bilateral Brain Stimulation (not a point)
SH	Side of Hand

First Time Through

Think about areas in life you struggle to have hope while using your fingertips to tap 3-5 times on each point in the algorithm.

When you get to BH+B(30), tap the BH continuously while stepping back and forth or moving your eyes side to side for at least 30 seconds. The B stands for bilateral, so you are trying to get bilateral brain stimulation going by doing things that cross the vertical hemisphere of the body.

Second Time Through

After you've gone through the points focusing on clearing hopelessness, you can go back through the points again focusing on being filled with hope, seeing new opportunities, confident that good things are in your future.

Third Time Through

Meditate on this verse as you tap through the points a third time:

> *"May the God of hope fill you with all joy and peace as you trust in him, so that you may overflow with hope by the power of the Holy Spirit."*
>
> Romans 15:13 (NIV)

Repeat this tapping algorithm a few times a day, especially when you are struggling with hopelessness.

This Month's Tapping Video

URL and Password are both case sensitive

http://bit.ly/HebrewMonthsTapping

Password: RipeInEachSeason

Iyar אייר

Starts in April or May

The month of Iyar is known as the month of natural healing. The word Iyar, is actually a Hebrew acronym taken from Exodus 15:26, "I Am the Lord your healer." It's also the verse where we get Jehovah Rapha, the Lord your healer, as a name of God. As you work through emotional healing this month it is also a good time to rest in Jehovah Rapha and pray for healing in the physical.

Iyar is also associated with light. Many places in scripture call this month Ziv, meaning radiance. Pay special attention this month to the Light of the World shining from you. Despite what the news may lead us to believe, light is winning, the world is getting better, not worse, as the Kingdom advances (Check out *Why You've Been Duped Into Believing That The World Is Getting Worse* by J.D. King if you want the stats to back up your hope).

Though commonly celebrated on the Thursday forty days from Easter, the day of Jesus' accension was on the fortieth day of counting the Omer from Passover, the 24th of Iyar. Resurrected at the beginning of the First Fruits barely harvest, and ascended at the end of the this first harvest. Barley is regarded as a grain for the poor, or common person. Like the feeding of the 5,000 from two barley loaves (Matthew 14:13-21), our Saviour is abundantly enough for all of humanity.

Iyar is when the Israelites were first in the desert and without water. They came upon water but it was bitter. So God had Moses throw a tree into the water and it became sweet

> *Then Moses led Israel from the Red Sea, and they went out into the wilderness of Shur; and they went three days in the wilderness and found no water. When they came to Marah, they could not drink the waters of Marah, for they were bitter; therefore it was named Marah.*
>
> *So the people grumbled at Moses, saying, "What shall we drink?" Then he cried out to the Lord, and the Lord showed him a tree; and he threw it into the waters, and the waters became sweet.*
>
> *There He made for them a statute and regulation, and there He tested them. And He said, "If you will give earnest heed to the voice of the Lord your God, and do what is right in His sight, and give ear to His commandments, and keep all His statutes, I will put none of the diseases on you which I*

have put on the Egyptians; for I, the Lord, am your healer.

Exodus 15:22-26 (NASB)

The interesting thing about bitterness in scripture is that it isn't always talking about bitterness like we typically think of it — unforgiveness, resentment, or anger. Often when a verse mentions bitterness it is talking about deep emotional pain, crushed in spirit, torment of the soul.

Trauma isn't discussed in scripture with the terms we use in modern thinking; instead bitterness is used in many instances where we would say trauma or emotional pain. Which is very important to keep in mind as you read Ruth 1:20 that Naomi changed her name to Mara — meaning bitter. It was during Iyar that Ruth and Naomi made their trek back to Israel from Moab and Naomi declared this bitter identity.

How often do we let our bitterness shape our identity? How often do we let the painful stories in our lives bring shame? As we work on releasing bitterness this month, let yourself think of bitterness in ways you may not have before. Think about the painful experiences you've had in life that have made you feel like hiding. The moments that felt so devastating that, like Naomi, made you feel like your very identity had changed.

God had Moses and the Israelites throw a tree into the bitter water to make it sweet. We have Jesus, the Oak of Righteousness (Luke 4), to turn sweet the bitter experiences of our lives, remove the shame, restore our true identities, and bring redemption to the worst parts of our stories.

Our God of redemption and second chances even planned for a second chance at partaking in Passover. In Numbers 9, he instructs Moses to have anyone who was unclean or away on a journey during Passover to observe the holiday on the same days the next month, Iyar. If you missed celebrating Passover this year flip back to the Nisan chapter for some ideas on how to observe it for Second Passover.

This month's body part is the right kidney. The right kidney can symbolize introspection and some emotions associated with it are shame, dread, regret, and being traumatized. The kidney meridian is active from 5-7 p.m. so pay attention to emotions that are heightened at that time.

I'm praying for you this month that God would strip back the lenses of identity that have come from pain and give you eyes to see yourself as he sees you. For second chances to enjoy the blessings God had intended for you and a restoration of anything lost or stolen by trauma. I'm praying also for your physical healing, that this would be a month of breakthrough in healing both naturally and supernaturally.

Other Scripture References to Iyar

Exodus 16

Numbers 1:1, 18; 9:11; 10:11

Numbers 3 (According to Jasher)

1 Kings 6:1, 37

1 Chronicles 27:4

2 Chronicles 3:2; 30

Ezra 3:8

Ruth 1:22; 2

2 Samuel 21:9

1 Chronicles 11:13

Mark 16:19-20

Luke 24:49-53

Acts 1:6-11

Iyar Tapping

CTT Exercise for Redemption:

EB-E-A-PF-IF-MF-CB-BH+B(30)-SH

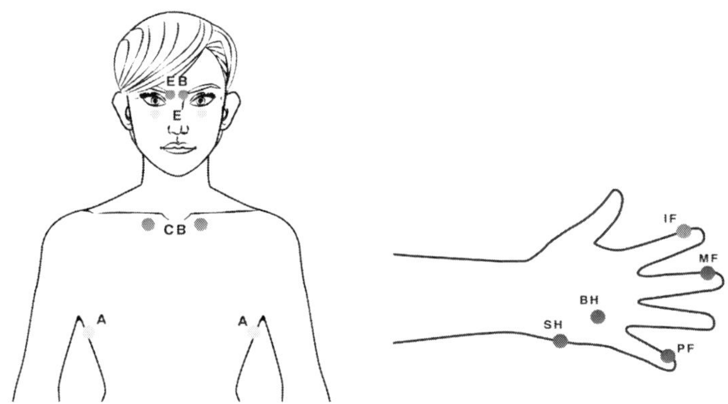

Tapping Points

EB	Eyebrows
E	Under Eyes
A	Under Arms
PF	Pinkie Finger
IF	Index Finger
MF	Middle Finger
CB	Collarbones
BH	Back of Hand
B	Bilateral Brain Stimulation (not a point)
SH	Side of Hand

First Time Through

Think about the bitterness, what it feels like, and what happened to cause it while using your fingertips to tap 3-5 times on each point in the algorithm.

When you get to BH+B(30), tap the BH continuously while stepping back and forth or moving your eyes side to side for at least 30 seconds. The B stands for bilateral, so you are trying to get bilateral brain stimulation going by doing things that cross the vertical hemisphere of the body.

Second Time Through

After you've gone through the points focusing on clearing bitterness, you can go back through the points again focusing on the bitter being made sweet—God redeeming every hurt, every trauma, every bitter experience.

Third Time Through

Meditate on these verses as you tap through the points a third time:

> *I cried out to you in my distress, the delivering God, and from your temple-throne you heard my troubled cry. My sobs came right into your heart and you turned your face to rescue me.*
>
> Psalm 18:6 (TPT)

> *You called out to me in your time of trouble and I rescued you. I came down from the realm of the secret place of thunder where mysteries hide. I came down to save you. I tested your hearts at the place where there was no water to drink, the place of your bitter argument with me.*
>
> Psalm 81:7 (TPT)

Repeat this tapping algorithm a few times a day, especially when you are feeling bitter or remembering events of the past you feel bitter about.

This Month's Tapping Video

URL and Password are both case sensitive

http://bit.ly/HebrewMonthsTapping

Password: RipeInEachSeason

Sivan סיון

Starts in May or June

The month of Sivan is known as the month of giving, alignment, and mercy. Sivan is when Moses received the Torah and Ten Commandments on Mt. Sinai and it is also when the disciples received the Holy Spirit during Pentecost.

We see in Exodus:19-20 that God's desire was to reveal himself to all of Israel, not just Moses. He instructed them to consecrate themselves in preparation and that on the 3rd of Sivan he would come down for Mount Sinai for all to see and hear him. Unfortunately the people of Israel gave into fear and insisted Moses serve as an intermediary for them instead of seeing and hearing God directly for themselves.

Even in the Old Testament, God's desire was to give himself to his people, to communicate with them directly so they could live in alignment with him.

The offer that Israel rejected was again extended to the disciples on Pentecost – *you can hear and see God for yourself.* Only now through Jesus' resurrection we can not only have access to God, we can have Holy Spirit constantly indwelling with us.

Sadly like Israel, Christians today have often rejected God's offer. Fear of the Holy Spirit has left many Christians relying on an intermediary of their pastor or other faith leader instead of hearing from God as directly as possible. While there is certainly a place for leaders and teachers, God's desire is for direct, intimate relationship with all of his people.

Pentecost is also known as Shavout or the Feast of Weeks (15 Sivan). Shavout marks seven weeks and fifty days from the second day of Passover (50 days counting the Omer) and the beginning of the wheat harvest (Leviticus 23:15-16). On Shavout the people would gather together for offerings and a sabbath, which is likely why the disciples were all together on the day we now know as Pentecost.

Sivan's body part is the left foot. Spleen and stomach points are associated with the left foot and some emotions associated with them are worry, despair, apathy, and selfishness. The spleen meridian is active from 9-11 a.m. so you may notice these emotions more strongly then. The left side of the body is also associated with the feminine and the feet with feeling supported. This may be a season to examine wounds you have from relationships with the women in your life or ways you are needing support.

The emotional focus this month is generosity, not just the act of giving but cultivating a generous spirit. Generosity is all about alignment with the heart of God. When we align with his heart, we don't fear scarcity; we are able to give freely from a place of abundance. When we're aligned with his heart, we also are able to trust in his justice and extend mercy and forgiveness freely.

> *The generous person will be prosperous, And he who waters will himself be watered.*
>
> Proverbs 11:25 (NASB)

In Ruth chapter 2 we see how Boaz's generosity during the wheat harvest provided for Ruth and Naomi. Not only did Boaz allow Ruth to glean behind his workers in the field as the law instructed (Leviticus 23:22), but he also provided her protection, allowing her to glean alongside his workers in safety and abundance.

Sivan is also associated with walking out the things you have talked about. Whatever the dreams, plans, or goals are that you've been talking about the past few months, now is the time to take action towards them. When we align ourselves with God's heart, and let generosity flow we find that there is more than enough for our needs as well. As you walk out what you've talked about, know that a generous heart is key to seeing the breakthroughs.

In Esther chapter 8 we see how action was set in motion on the 23rd of Sivan for the Jewish people to not only defend themselves, but plunder the enemy of all that was stolen from them. Take note of "decrees" this month and what God is setting in motion for your benefit.

I'm praying for you in Sivan that God would uproot the fears that have held back in your relationship with him and in your generosity. That you would be aligned with the full knowledge of the abundance of an open heaven. That you would get a fresh anointing of Holy Spirit as we enter the Pentecost season. And that you would prosper in every part of life (not just financially) as you walk in alignment with God's generous heart–living from glory-to-glory instead of pay check-to-pay check.

Other Scripture References to Sivan

Exodus 19; 24; 31; 34:22

Leviticus 23:15-16

Judges 15:1

Ruth 2

1 Samuel 6:13; 12:17;

1 Chronicles 21:20-23; 27:5

2 Chronicles 15:10; 31:7

Esther 8:9

Ezekiel 31:1

Acts 2:1-38

Sivan Tapping

CTT Exercise for Generosity:

E – A – CB – BH+B(30) – SH

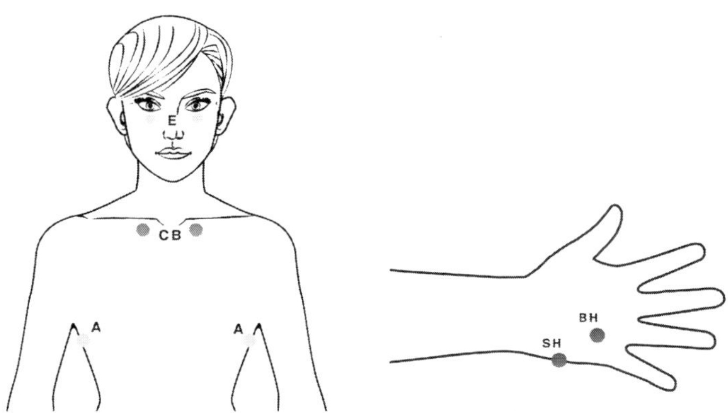

Tapping Points

E Under Eyes
A Under Arms
CB Collarbones
BH Back of Hand
B Bilateral Brain Stimulation (not a point)
SH Side of Hand

First Time Through

Think about any fears or feelings that hold you back from being generous while using your fingertips to tap 3-5 times on each point in the algorithm.

When you get to BH+B(30), tap the BH continuously while stepping back and forth or moving your eyes side to side for at least 30 seconds. The B stands for bilateral, so you are trying to get bilateral brain stimulation going by doing things that cross the vertical hemisphere of the body.

Second Time Through

After you've gone through the points focusing on clearing blocks to generosity, you go back through the points again focusing on being filled with generosity, mercy, an open heart, and sense of abundance.

Third Time Through

Meditate on this verse as you tap through the points a third time:

> *The generous person will be prosperous, And he who waters will himself be watered.*
>
> Proverbs 11:25 (NASB)

Repeat this tapping algorithm a few times a day, especially when you are struggling to feel generous.

This Month's Tapping Video

URL and Password are both case sensitive

http://bit.ly/HebrewMonthsTapping

Password: RipeInEachSeason

Tammuz תמוז

Starts in June or July

The month of Tammuz is known as the month of worship, vision, and covenant. Tammuz is when the Israelites made a golden calf to worship when they feared Moses would not return off Mt. Sinai (Exodus 32). And it's also when Caleb, Joshua, and the other ten spies searched out the Promised Land (Numbers 13:1-24). The name of the month comes from the Babylonian captivity and is actually a Babylonian god, highlighting again how important it is for us to worship the true God (Ezekiel 8:14).

Tammuz is a time to take notice of where you've set your vision. Joshua, Caleb, and the other ten spies all witnessed both the giants and the abundant fruit in the Promised Land, but when they arrived back in Av to give their report, only Joshua and Caleb had their gaze set on the fruit and the promise God had made to give it to them. Where we set our vision impacts how and whom we worship with our hearts and lives. Are the giants or God bigger in your eyes?

Joshua's gaze was so fixed on God, that years later on the 3rd of Tammuz, he commanded in faith that the sun and moon stand still to allow Israel to defeat the Amorites, and they did for about a full day! In adoration, he believed that God meant it when he said he had given Israel victory and not to be afraid (Joshua 10:1-15). Joshua knew the land God had promised Israel, he knew the promise God had given in that battle, and his belief in those promises shaped how he responded when he faced opposition. What promises has God made to you? What prophetic words have you been given that you need to revisit?

Worship was a central issue in another event that likely happened during Tammuz. David came to bring his brothers bread and grain when he heard Goliath taunt the armies of Israel and mocking God. While the armies shuddered with fear, David demanded, "Just who is this uncircumcised Philistine that he should defy the armies of the living God?" (1 Samuel 17:26 HCSB). Circumcision was a mark of worship and submission to God; David was not upset to hear the army taunted, he heard Goliath's challenge as an insulting defiance of the one true God. Defeating Goliath wasn't just a military victory, it was a declaration of who is worthy of worship.

The 17th of Tammuz is regarded as the day Moses came down with the first set of Ten Commandment tablets and found Israel worshipping the golden calf. On the 9th of Tammuz centuries later, the Babylonians under Nebuchadnezzar breached the walls of Jerusalem and began to destroy the city, leading to the destruction of the 1st Temple on the

9th of Av. This same Nebuchadnezzar carried off the youth of Israel, notably Hananiah, Azariah, and Mishael, or as you may better know them – Shadrach, Meshach, and Abednego the three young men that refused to bow in worship to Nebuchadnezzar. The 17th of Tammuz is significant again in 70A.D./3830 when the walls of Jerusalem were breached by the Roman army, leading to the destruction of the 2nd Temple.

Zechariah 8:19 references a "fast of the fourth month" which modern Rabbinical teaching regards at the 17th of Tammuz, a day to mourn the breach of the walls of Jerusalem. This can be a good day to devote to worship and fasting, turning your heart and stomach's longings towards the Lord. There are patterns over and over of what was set in motion in Tammuz continuing to fruition in Av. We head in the direction of our gaze; keep your gaze fixed on Jesus in this month especially.

For Tammuz the body part is the right hand. Large intestine and heart points are associated with the right hand and some emotions associated with them are rejection, envy, sadness, confusion, and nightmares. (Yes, nightmares aren't exactly an emotion but we certainly do feel them.) The heart meridian is active from 11 a.m. to 1 p.m. so take time to do this month's tapping exercise during your lunch break.

The right hand also has significance in scripture as being a symbol of righteousness.

> *Do not fear, for I am with you; Do not anxiously look about you, for I am your God. I will strengthen you, surely I will help you, Surely I will uphold you with My righteous right hand.*
>
> Isaiah 41:10 (NASB)

Pay attention this month to the covenants, the agreements you make, the things you shake on. Are those agreements in line with the vision you want to set? With the righteousness you are called to?

The emotion we are focusing on this month is adoration. When we are filled with adoration, we can't help but worship and see despair flee. As you tap this month, be sure to take extra time to worship each day as well. Worship doesn't have to be music; it's the heart posture we take when we respond in adoration in any part of our lives.

I'm praying for you this month that God would remove lies that have clouded your vision and trapped you in despair. That the giants in your Promised Land would be made small in your eyes. That you would rest in worship and the renewing of covenant with the Lord that our hearts make every time we worship.

Two really great songs to rest in this month are *Surrounded* and *Defender* both by Upperroom.

Other Scripture References to Tammuz

Genesis 8:5; 30:14

Joshua 10:1-15

Ruth 3

1 Samuel 17

2 Kings 25:3

1 Chronicles 27:7

Jeremiah 39:2; 52:6

Ezekiel 1-3

Tammuz Tapping

CTT Exercise for Adoration:

E – UN – IF – MF – BH+B(30) – SH

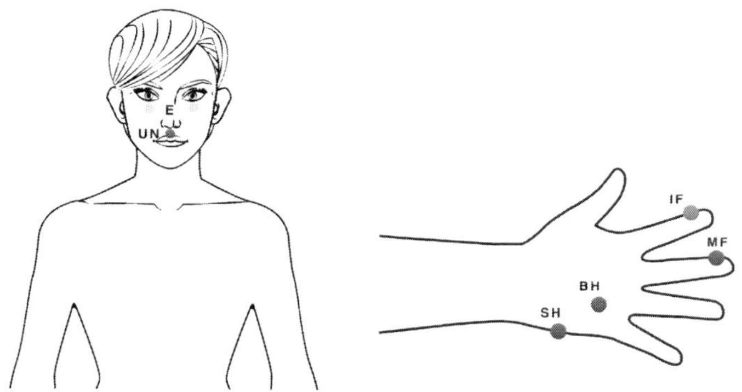

Tapping Points

E	Under Eyes
UN	Under Nose
IF	Index Finger
MF	Middle Finger
BH	Back of Hand
B	Bilateral Brain Stimulation (not a point)
SH	Side of Hand

First Time Through

Think about the places you feel despair in your life, where the giants in the promised land seem too big while using your fingertips to tap 3-5 times on each point in the algorithm.

When you get to BH+B(30), tap the BH continuously while stepping back and forth or moving your eyes side to side for at least 30 seconds. The B stands for bilateral, so you are trying to get bilateral brain stimulation going by doing things that cross the vertical hemisphere of the body.

Second Time Through

After you've gone through the points focusing on clearing despair, go back through the points again focusing on being filled with adoration, a heart of worship, and having your vision set on Jesus.

Third Time Through

Meditate on this verse as you tap through the points a third time:

> *"I am covered by your covenant of mercy and love. So I come to your sanctuary with deepest awe to bow in worship and adore you."*
>
> Psalm 5:7 (TPT)

Repeat this tapping algorithm a few times a day, especially when you are struggling with despair.

This Month's Tapping Video

URL and Password are both case sensitive

http://bit.ly/HebrewMonthsTapping

Password: RipeInEachSeason

Av אב

Starts in July or August

Av was destined to be the season of entering promised lands but instead became the low point in the Hebrew year. It's the month when the spies returned from the Promised Land giving a bad report, and Israel refused to receive the blessing God had planned for them (Numbers 13:25-33; 14)

For months Israel had followed Moses out of Egypt and into the desert. There had already been quite a lot of complaining even though God had provided for them the whole way. If you read carefully through Exodus, you'll notice God hadn't really told them much about the promised land. It had been 400 years since Abraham lived in Canaan, no one remembered what it was like there (Genesis 15:15-21). They only had rumours of oral tradition and imagination to inform their idea of what the promised land held. The only thing God had told Moses and Israel specifically is that he would give the land to them and that is was a good place he was bringing them to out of Egypt.

Why do you think God told Moses to send spies into the land? For military intelligence on how to conquer it? God already said he was giving it to them, and his track record with Egypt was pretty good on giving them the information and instructions they needed. For them to see the giants in the land and decide if the fight was worth it? Clearly God intended to give it to them regardless of the current occupants.

I believe God had Moses send spies to see the abundance of the land, the flowing milk and honey, the fertile soil, the beauty not seen by their ancestors for centuries. He sent them to whet their appetites. What promised lands has God sent you to spy out? Are you focused on the obstacles or on the abundance that he's offering to give you? Are you growing in hunger for the things of God?

As you read through Leviticus, Deuteronomy, and Numbers, keep in mind God gave all of these commandments to a nomadic people. Moses was writing about wheat harvests and new wine while the Israelites wandered the desert eating manna and quail. In the wilderness God was preparing them for a time when they would have abundance. Perhaps God is preparing you in this season for the blessings ahead. Most lottery winners go broke within five years of winning. Having abundance does not guarantee success, and abundance comes in many forms other than dollar signs. We must learn to steward the blessings God sends our way, and he is faithful to prepare us if we will allow him to do so.

Historically Av has been a tragic month for the Jewish people ever since, with the destruction of the first and second temples and significant events during the Holocaust; all occurring on the 9th of Av (Tish'a B'Av) the date the spies returned with bad report.

The destruction of the 2nd Temple in 70 A.D. created a problem for the people of Israel. *How do we offer sacrifices to cover our sins without a temple?* Jesus' death and resurrection was the final sacrifice, marked by the tearing of the temple curtain from top to bottom (Matthew 27:51). But without a temple and without recognizing Christ's final sacrifice, the Jewish leaders created their own way to atone for sins and restore relationship with God: good works, repentance, and prayer. A familiar formula to all that try to achieve righteousness apart from Jesus.

The first portion of Av is considered a time of mourning, followed by seven weeks of comfort starting on the 10th of Av. This is a season of the old stuff that's not working being destroyed so the new can be rebuilt. It's also regarded as a month of growing in discernment. Pay attention this month to what old is falling away and what new God is building. It takes discernment to know when it is God pruning versus when it is spiritual attack.

Av is associated with the left kidney. Mirroring the right kidney in Iyar, some other emotions that are associated with the kidneys are performance mentality, fear, and feeling stuck. Again, the kidney meridian is active from 5-7 p.m. so pay extra attention to these emotions if you feel them at that time.

So much of Av's history is negative, but that is not its destiny. Do not be afraid that this month will be a low point for you. Reject the mournful history of this season and lay claim to the original intent of this being a season of entering into blessing.

I'm praying for you this month that God would deepen your discernment and help you see where he's been at work that you were unaware. That when you are given a bad report about your Promised Lands you would have the discernment to know what is actually true and what voices to listen to. And that you would lean into the ways he is preparing you for what is ahead.

Other Scripture References to Av

Numbers 13:20; 33:38

Judges 9:27

2 Kings 25:8-21

1 Chronicles 27:8

Ezra 7:8-9

Nehemiah 3:1; 6:15

Jeremiah 28:1; 52:12

Ezekiel 20:1

Zechariah 7:3

Other Date of Note

3 Av, Feast of New Wine

Av Tapping

CTT Exercise for Discernment:

EB – T – A – PF – BH+B(30) – SH

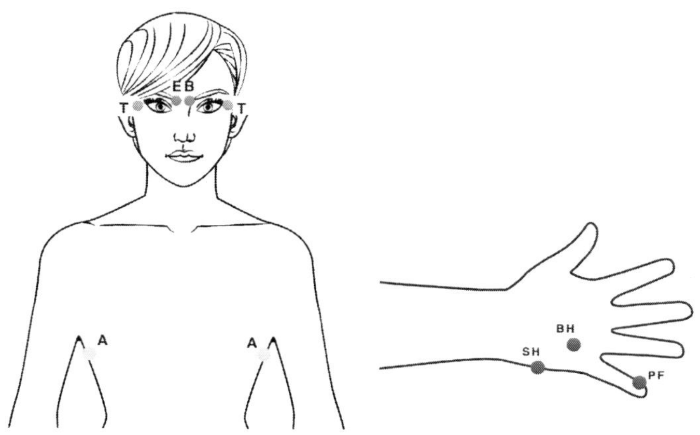

Tapping Points

EB	Eyebrows
T	Temples
A	Under Arms
PF	Pinkie Finger
BH	Back of Hand
B	Bilateral Brain Stimulation (not a point)
SH	Side of Hand

First Time Through

Think about the places you feel confusion and lack of clarity, where you struggle to believe the promises God's given you are true while using your fingertips to tap 3-5 times on each point in the algorithm.

When you get to BH+B(30), tap the BH continuously while stepping back and forth or moving your eyes side to side for at least 30 seconds. The B stands for bilateral, so you are trying to get bilateral brain stimulation going by doing things that cross the vertical hemisphere of the body.

Second Time Through

After you've gone through the points focusing on clearing out the negative, go back through the points again focusing on being filled with discernment, clarity, and connection with Holy Spirit.

Third Time Through

Meditate on this verse as you tap through the points a third time:

"Teach me good discernment and knowledge, for I believe in Your commandments."

Psalm 119:66 (NASB)

Repeat this tapping algorithm a few times a day, especially when you are struggling with lack of discernment.

This Month's Tapping Video

URL and Password are both case sensitive

http://bit.ly/HebrewMonthsTapping

Password: RipeInEachSeason

Elul אלול

Starts in August or September

Ani L'dodi, V'dodi li — I am my beloved's and my beloved is mine.

Song of Solomon 6:3 (TLV)

Elul is actually a Hebrew acronym taken from this well-loved verse. Even in its name, Elul brings a spirit of intimacy.

This month is known as the season "*the king is in the field*"(2 Chronicles 19:4). It was a time when the king would come down from his palace, past all the barriers that usually prevent access to him, and would set up a tent in the fields so anyone who desired could come and meet with him. It's a beautiful foreshadowing of the access and intimacy Jesus restored to us through the cross. The veil is torn; we no longer have to wait for the king to be in the field (Matthew 27:51).

Take some extra time this month to just sit with your Beloved. Don't let the usual requirements of visiting the king in his palace get in the way. The King is in the field. What are the fields— the common places in your life— he wants to show up this month?

The end of Elul marks the New Oil (22 Elul) and Wood offerings (23-28 Elul). The Dead Sea Scrolls record the timing of these offerings that Leviticus and Deuteronomy describe but do not date. Oil is a symbol of God's presence, the Holy Spirit, and anointing. Wood was required for every burnt offering throughout the year and is a symbol of salvation – Noah's Ark, the Ark of the Covenant, and the Cross of Christ were all made of wood. With these two offerings we see a picture of God's plan for intimacy with us through his presence and salvation.

Elul precedes the Day of Atonement — Yom Kippur. What's important about this is that Yom Kippur is when sacrifices were made to atone for sins. Sin is what separates us from God and gets in the way of relationship with him, but even before the Day of Atonement, God was showing us that he is the one coming to us. He is the one making the way of atonement and restoring our access to him. While Elul is known as a season of repentance, mercy, and forgiveness, preparing for Yom Kippur— keep in mind this is all in the context of the King of Kings coming to us.

Ezekiel 8:1-11:25 gives another glimpse of our King's desire to restore connection with us. Ezekiel describes a vision he had during the month of Elul. It is a long and complex vision, but what stands out is God's search for people that mourn the detestable things being done in Israel and his plan, "to remove from them [the people of Israel] their heart of stone and give them a heart of flesh" (Ezekiel 11:19). God sees the detestable things done in our day and mourns them along with you. He is still in the business of turning hearts of stone into hearts of flesh.

Another prophetic word came on the 1st of Elul a through Haggai that it was time to finish rebuilding the temple (Haggai 1:1-15). When the Israelites had first arrived back in Israel Zerubbabel the governor of Judah and Joshua the high priest had set to work immediately building the foundations of the Second Temple. There was opposition to their work and ultimately the Persians who were financing it pulled their support and the temple work stopped (Ezra 4).

The foundations sat for seventeen years while Israel rebuilt their homes, neglecting the Lord's. With Haggai's word, the people's spirits were stirred and they were quick to obey God's command to build, beginning the work on the 24th of Elul that same year (Ezra 5:1-2). God is seeking those whose spirits are stirred by his word, who hear his voice and are quick to obey.

Elul is full of symbolism declaring God's desire for a people holy people with whom he can share the intimate places of his heart and his dedicated pursuit of his beloved. Pay special attention in this season to lean into the heart of God, to allow him to turn your stony parts to flesh, to listen carefully for his voice and quickly obey when you hear him as your personal spirit is stirred by the Holy Spirit.

For Elul the body part is the left-hand. The small intestine meridian is associated with the hand and some related emotions are vulnerability, heartbreak, insecurity, and denial. The small intestine meridian is active from 1-3 p.m. so be sure to connect with Jesus in this time and invite his intimacy to heal those wounds.

I'm praying for you this month that your eyes would be open to see The King in your fields. That any shame, lies, or pretence that have been holding you back from the intimacy you desire with Him would fall away and you'd find new levels of intimacy with Him. That your personal spirit would buzz with life as you receive clear revelations from God and that you would be quick to obey when you hear his direction.

Other Scripture References to Elul

1 Chronicles 27:9

Ezra 5

Ezekiel 8:1-11:25

Haggai 1:1-15

Elul Tapping

CTT Exercise for Intimacy:

TH – EB – UN – MF – BH+B(30) – SH

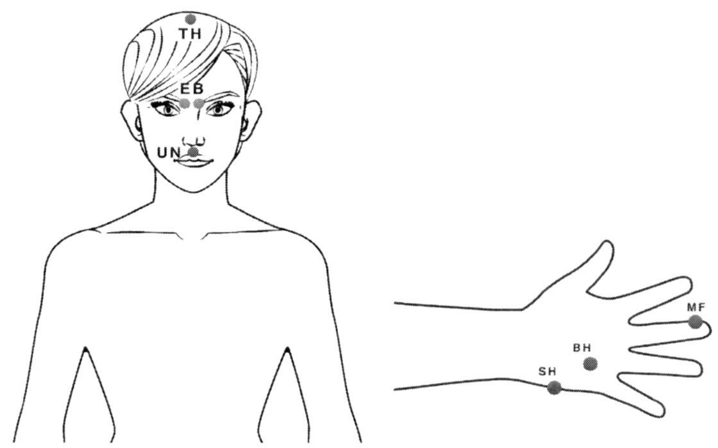

Tapping Points

TH	Top of Head
EB	Eyebrows
UN	Under Nose
MF	Middle Finger
BH	Back of Hand
B	Bilateral Brain Stimulation (not a point)
SH	Side of Hand

First Time Through

Think about any ways you feel a lack of intimacy with God or he feels distant while using your fingertips to tap 3-5 times on each point in the algorithm.

When you get to BH+B(30), tap the BH continuously while stepping back and forth or moving your eyes side to side for at least 30 seconds. The B stands for bilateral, so you are trying to get bilateral brain stimulation going by doing things that cross the vertical hemisphere of the body.

Second Time Through

After you've gone through the points focusing on lack of intimacy, go back through the points again focusing on being filled with intimacy, intimacy feeling safe, being able to feel close to God and others.

Third Time Through

Meditate on this verse as you tap through the points a third time:

I am my beloved's and my beloved is mine.

Song of Solomon 6:3 (NASB)

Repeat this tapping algorithm a few times a day, especially when you are struggling with lack of intimacy.

This Month's Tapping Video

URL and Password are both case sensitive

http://bit.ly/HebrewMonthsTapping
Password: RipeInEachSeason

Tishrei תשרי

Starts in September or October

The 1st of Tishrei marks the beginning of Rosh Hashanah, the Jewish civil New Year. It's also the beginning of the High Holy Days with Yom Kippur on the 10th of Tishrei, and Sukkot beginning on the 15th of Tishrei. And every seven years, marks the beginning of the Shemitah year rest. All of these holidays have significance for us even on this side of the new covenant.

Rosh Hashanah is celebrated by the sounding of the shofar and eating apples dipped in honey to symbolize a sweet New Year. You won't find any reference to Rosh Hashanah (Head of the Year) in scripture though, this first day of Tishrei is known in the Bible as Yom Teruah, the Day of Shouting (Leviticus 23:23-25; Numbers 29:1-6).

Leviticus describes Yom Teruah as a special sabbath, a day of rest. Other than blowing the shofar, this isn't a day that is filled with lots of rituals and activity. Tishrei is the seventh month so it is commonly associated with the seventh day of creation and the rest God established as a pattern for us to follow.

Though not specifically stated in scripture, it has long been tradition to sound the shofar 100 times on Yom Teruah. Fortunately you aren't expected to blow the shofar yourself, as long as you hear it blown. It's unclear why God commanded this rest begin with shouting and blowing the shofar but the blasts of the shofar itself may give us some clues.

There are different types of shofar blasts each with a special meaning:

- Tekiah: one long note, serves as a call to worship
- Shevarim: three medium notes, means “to break”, “to fracture”, or “to repent”
- T’ruah: series of very short notes, like sounding an alarm

Hear the different shofar blasts
www.healinginthehebrewmonths.com/shofar

Reasons we Blow the Shofar

- To announce the Messiah
- To chase away the devil
- To wake us from our spiritual slumber

Each of the shofar blasts matches up with these reasons for blowing it. Tekiah with announcing the

Messiah (1 Thessalonians 4:15-17). Shevarim with chasing away the devil, breaking him off. And T'ruah with waking us up from our spiritual slumber.

On Rosh Hashanah/Yom Teruah you'll often hear all three of these shofar blasts in different combinations, which often end with a longer variation of Tekiah called Tekiah Gadolah.

From the rest of Yom Teruah, we enter into Yom Kippur, the Day of Atonement. It's speculated by many scholars that Jesus was actually born on Yom Kippur, symbolizing his ultimate atonement and our ultimate security in our salvation.

Finally, with Sukkot, the Feast of Tabernacles, we are reminded of God's provision in wilderness seasons when temporary tents were our only protection. The feast of tabernacles also foreshadows the coming of the Holy Spirit who now dwells in each of us as individual tabernacles. Our personal spirits can rest securely knowing they are provided for and guided by the Holy Spirit.

The reproductive organs are associated with Tishrei and some emotions connected with them are paranoia, insecurity, exhaustion, self-sabotage, and vulnerability. This meridian is active from 7-9 p.m. so you may find these emotions expressing more strongly then.

Take some extra time this month reflecting on the security you have through Jesus' atonement. You can have security in your identity, your relationships, your salvation, your peace of mind – all because of his atonement.

I'll be praying for you this month that your spirit, mind, and body would rest securely. Your borders are at peace and your needs are provided for (Psalm 147:14). You are safe to rest and rejoice.

Other Scripture References to Tishrei

Genesis 28:10-22 (According to Jubilees)

Leviticus 16:29; 23:24-27, 34, 39, 41; 25:9

Numbers 29:1, 7, 12

Deuteronomy 16:13, 16; 31:10

Joshua 13-20

1 Samuel 1:21

1 Kings 8:2

2 Kings 25:25

1 Chronicles 27:10

2 Chronicles 5:3; 7:10; 8: 13; 31:7

Ezra 3:1-6; 6

Nehemiah 7:73; 8:2, 13-14

Jeremiah 28:17; 41:1

Ezekiel 45:25

Daniel 5:13-30

Haggai 2:1-9

Zechariah 7:5; 14:16-19

Luke 2:1-10

John 7, 8

Acts 27:9

Tishrei Tapping

CTT Exercise for Security:

TH - EB - CB - MF - PF - BH+B(30) - SH

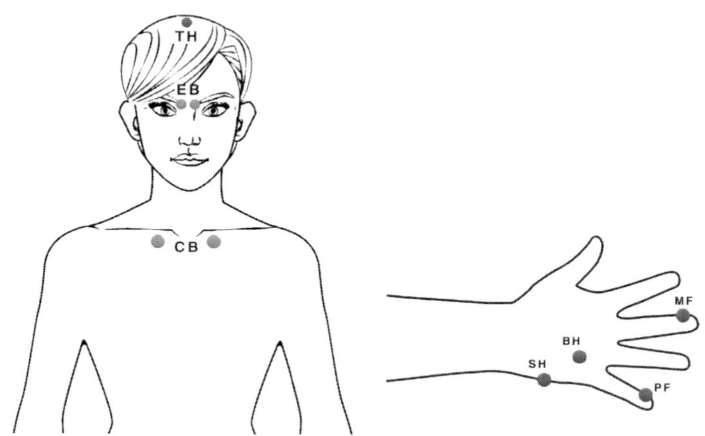

Tapping Points

TH Top of Head
EB Eyebrows
CB Collarbones
MF Middle Finger
PF Pinkie Finger
BH Back of Hand
B Bilateral Brain Stimulation (not a point)
SH Side of Hand

First Time Through

Think about any ways you feel insecure, in your identity, physical safety, relationships, finances, any area of life you feel security is lacking, while using your fingertips to tap 3-5 times on each point in the algorithm.

When you get to BH+B(30), tap the BH continuously while stepping back and forth or moving your eyes side to side for at least 30 seconds. The B stands for bilateral, so you are trying to get bilateral brain stimulation going by doing things that cross the vertical hemisphere of the body.

Second Time Through

After you've gone through the points focusing on lack of security, go back through the points again focusing on feeling secure in your identity, your relationships, your future, your present. Invite Holy Spirit to fill in those places of insecurity with the security we have in him.

Third Time Through

Meditate on this verse as you tap through the points a third time:

> *"Therefore my heart is glad and my spirit rejoices; my body also rests securely."*
>
> Psalm 16:9 (HCSB)

Repeat this tapping algorithm a few times a day, especially when you are struggling with feeling insecure.

This Month's Tapping Video

URL and Password are both case sensitive

http://bit.ly/HebrewMonthsTapping

Password: RipeInEachSeason

Cheshvan חשון

Starts in October or November

Don't you say, 'There are still four more months, then comes the harvest'? Listen to what I'm telling you: Open your eyes and look at the fields, for they are ready for harvest.

John 4:35 (HCSB)

In North American agriculture, we typically think of harvest in the Fall, yet in Israel the harvest began in Spring. Cheshvan, the end of the Autumn months, is actually when the harvest was over – four months until it would begin again in Spring. This saying, "four months yet until the harvest" seems to have been a sentiment of procrastination in Jesus' time. *The harvest isn't for another four months, we don't have to worry about that right now.* Yet Jesus pushed back against this cultural phrase, insisting that his Kingdom wasn't someday far off, but present and available now.

In this exchange Jesus is using harvest to describe people coming into the Kingdom. He uses this same language in Matthew 9:35-38 when he says, "The harvest is abundant, but the workers are few. Therefore, pray to the Lord of the harvest to send out workers into His harvest" (HCSB). And again in Mark 13 in the Parable of the Sower and the Parable of the Weeds. He makes the harvest even more personal in Matthew 21:33-43, when he presents himself as the Rejected Son coming to collect His Father's harvest – prophetically telling of his crucifixion. Harvest is a picture of revival, of evangelism, of sharing the good news about the Kingdom of God.

Harvest can also be seen as picture of Christ's return. Depending on your interpretation of Revelation, The Harvest of the Earth in chapter 14 is a spiritual picture of what was happening when Jesus was teaching about the harvest in Mark and Matthew, a prophetic picture of the harvest to come with his return, or both. Jesus often taught to be ready at all times for his return Matthew 24:36-44; Matthew 25:1-13

Cheshvan is the only month with no holidays, no feasts, no fasts. Traditionally it is believed Cheshvan is reserved as the month the Messiah will come. This month also plays a prominent role in the story of Noah; the flood both began and ended in the month of Cheshvan, marking the beginning of both cleansing and revelation.

> *For it will be exactly like it was in the days of Noah when the Son of Man appears. Before the flood, people lived their lives eating, drinking, marrying, and having children. They didn't realize the end was near until Noah entered the ark, and then suddenly, the flood came and took them all away in judgment. It will happen the same way when the Son of Man appears.*
>
> Matthew 24:37-39 (TPT)

In Noah's day were they saying, "four months yet until the harvest"? Like the Parable of the Virgins, were they letting their lamps dry up? Perhaps Jesus' rebuke about saying the harvest is still months away was not just about evangelism, but also about our own hearts, being always prepared for his return, always filled with the Holy Spirit, eager to bring even more harvest into his store house. Cheshvan marks four months until the harvest, but let us not live like the harvest is still far off.

The floodwaters cleansed the earth of unrighteousness, removing the old evil systems that had dominated. As the rain stopped and the water receded, there began a grand revelation of the new surface of the earth. Things hidden were revealed; new forms took shape. Everything Noah and his family used to know about navigating the world had been reshaped.

Cheshvan is a season of cleansing and revelation. It is a season of seeing deep roots that need healing as well as deep truths we haven't yet grasped. This is a great month to spend some time doing inner healing work, going after those roots — the roots of your pains, the roots of the lies that ensnare you, the roots of the automatic thoughts you can't escape. God doesn't reveal such roots until he's ready to heal them, so do not fear what you might find.

Revelation is the focus of the month, both in revealing what needs healing, and revealing greater truths and understanding to move forward.

I love how The Passion Translation talks about the book of Revelation being a revelation of Jesus Christ in his full glory. This month is a great time to read through Revelation and invite Holy Spirit to give you a greater revelation of Jesus. I highly recommend reading it in The Passion Translation as it brings a fresh view on this often-misunderstood book. The Passion Translation is free on the YouVersion Bible app.

For Cheshvan the body part is the intestines both large and small. Some associated emotions are discouragement, doubt, invalidated, trouble letting go, and shut down. The large intestine meridian is active from 5-7 a.m. and the small intestine meridian is active from 1-3 p.m.

Take some extra time this month reflecting on the security you have through Jesus' atonement. You can have security in your identity, your relationships, your salvation, your peace of mind — all because of his atonement.

I'm praying for you this month that your eyes will be open to greater revelation; that your heart will be prepared for whenever Messiah returns.

Other Scripture References to Cheshvan

Genesis 3 (According to Jubilees)

Genesis 7:11; 8:14

1 Kings 6:38; 12:32-33

1 Chronicles 27:11

Zechariah 1:1-6

Cheshvan Tapping

CTT Exercise for Revelation:

E – UN – IF – PF – BH+B(30) – SH

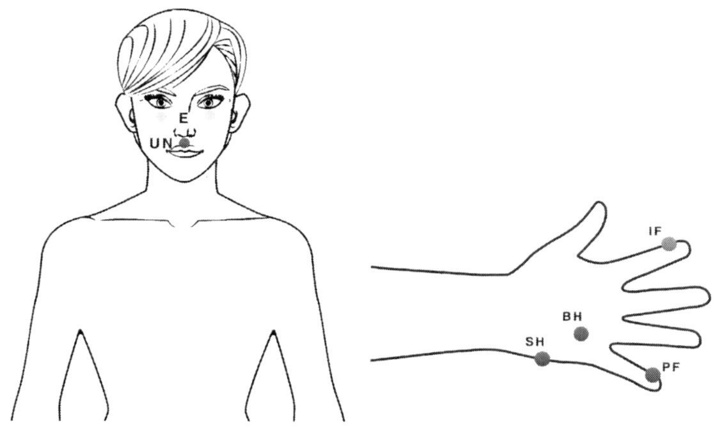

Tapping Points

E	Under Eyes
UN	Under Nose
IF	Index Finger
PF	Pinkie Finger
BH	Back of Hand
B	Bilateral Brain Stimulation (not a point)
SH	Side of Hand

First Time Through

Think about any ways you feel a lack of vision or understanding, while using your fingertips to tap 3-5 times on each point in the algorithm.

When you get to BH+B(30), tap the BH continuously while stepping back and forth or moving your eyes side to side for at least 30 seconds. The B stands for bilateral, so you are trying to get bilateral brain stimulation going by doing things that cross the vertical hemisphere of the body.

Second Time Through

After you've gone through the points focusing on lack of vision, go back through the points again focusing on having greater revelation and clarity, being open to whatever Holy Spirit wants to reveal.

Third Time Through

Meditate on this verse as you tap through the points a third time:

I pray that the Father of glory, the God of our Lord Jesus Christ, would impart to you the riches of the Spirit of wisdom and the Spirit of revelation to know him through your deepening intimacy with him.

Ephesians 1:16 (TPT)

Repeat this tapping algorithm a few times a day, especially when you are struggling with lack of vision.

This Month's Tapping Video

URL and Password are both case sensitive

http://bit.ly/HebrewMonthsTapping

Password: RipeInEachSeason

Kislev כסלו

Starts in November or December

Kislev is the season when the days progressively get darker. Its days have some of the shortest daylight hours, with the winter solstice falling near its end. Yet it's also the month that Hanukkah begins, the festival of lights. A reminder that *"the light shines in the darkness, and the darkness has not overcome it"* (John 1:5 NIV).

Though Hanukkah is often ignored by Christians, it actually is mentioned in John 10:22 as The Festival of Dedication and was celebrated by Jesus. At its core, Hanukkah is a celebration of the miraculous. In 168 B.C. Jerusalem was occupied by Syrians who desecrated the temple and set up idols of worship for Greek gods. The Jews came under extreme persecution, given the options of death or religious conversion. The head priest at the time was Mattathias, and his son Judah Maccabee became a leader among the Jewish people in resisting the Syrian army. The story of their revolt and the miracle of Hanukkah can be found in 1st and 2nd Maccabees[1], Apocryphal books that hold historical significance.

Despite extreme disadvantages, Judah Maccabee and his revolters were successful against the Syrians and after winning two major battles reclaimed control of the temple. After they removed the desecrations from the temple, they wanted to rededicate the temple to YHWH as soon as possible. But there was one problem, they did not have enough oil to keep the lampstand burning continuously. They only had enough for one night. The rituals to purify oneself for making the oil took seven days and then an additional day actually to make the oil. God had commanded that the lampstand always be burning, but they did not have enough to last the eight days needed to purify more oil.

Rather than dishonoring the process God had instructed them to follow, in their passion to light the lampstand immediately, they took a leap of faith and lit it with the little purified oil they had. Miraculously the lampstand continued to burn for an additional seven nights, long enough for them to ritually purify themselves and make more purified oil.

Hanukkah begins the 25th of Kislev and ends on the 2nd of Tevet. For more on celebrating this holiday check out my book *Miracles & Dedication: Christian Devotions for the Festival of Lights.*

Kislev also is known as the month of dreams because the Jewish traditional schedule of scripture readings for this time contains more passages regarding dreams than any other season. There's also a good chance Kislev is when Abraham had dreams that God would make his descendants as numerous as the stars (Genesis 15; 17), Joseph had his dreams that got him into trouble with his brothers (Genesis 37:5-10), and Jacob had a dream telling him it was safe to go to Egypt and reunite his family (Genesis 46). Kislev's long night hours make for a perfect season to sleep deeply. And dreaming is what we'll be focusing on cultivating this month.

Perhaps Mary also wondered if she was dreaming when Gabriel appeared to her announcing Jesus' conception. Counting from scholar's estimates of Jesus' birth, the events of Luke 1:26-56 likely happened during Kislev. Some years with the ebb and flow of Hebrew and Gregorian dates, December 25th aligns with Kislev. Could it be that we are celebrating Christ's conception with Christmas?

The name Kislev is said to come from the Hebrew root word *kecel* כֶּסֶל (Strongs H3688). Interestingly this word can be translated both as hope or foolishness. Just as the gospel may seem foolish to those that do not understand (1 Corinthians 1:18), our dreams may seem as foolishness to those the message of the dream is not for. But our dreams are a source of hope when we know that God is speaking to us through them.

Pay special attention to your dreams this month. It would be good to keep a journal and pen by your bedside to write them down as soon as you wake up. Dreams that may not seem significant when you first have them may reveal themselves to have more meaning as you look back at them later and ask God to show you what they mean.

Another exercise to engage in this month is coming up with 100 dreams for your life. Dreaming isn't just about dreams in the night, it's also about the dreams of our hearts. Spend some time writing down dreams you have for yourself – your family, your home, job, finances, fun, ministry, friendships, any and all areas of life. Keep pressing in until you have 100 dreams. Then go back through them and look for patterns.

Are there some areas of life you don't struggle to dream? Are there areas you have no dreams at all? Do you have some dreams that are totally beyond your control and ability? God-sized dreams that only he could fulfill? Spend time praying through the list you create asking God what he has to say about your dreams and what dreams he has for you.

Kislev is associated with the stomach. Some stomach meridian emotions are lack of trust, egotism, self-blame, hopelessness, and living vicariously. This meridian is active from 7-9 a.m., a perfect time to reflect on the dreams you had the night before.

I'm praying for you this month that you have dreams like never before. That the biggest God-sized dreams you can dream get expanded to even greater levels.

Other Scripture References to Kislev

Genesis 15; 17; 37:5-10; 46:1-27 (According to Jubilees)

1 Chronicles 27:12

Ezra 3:10-13; 9:1-15; 10:1-15

Nehemiah 1:1-11; 12-13

Jeremiah 36

Haggai 2:10-19

Zechariah 7:1-14

Matthew 1:18-25

Luke 1:26-56

John 10:22-23

Kislev Tapping

CTT Exercise for Dreaming:

TH - E - UN - CH - MF - BH+B(30) - SH

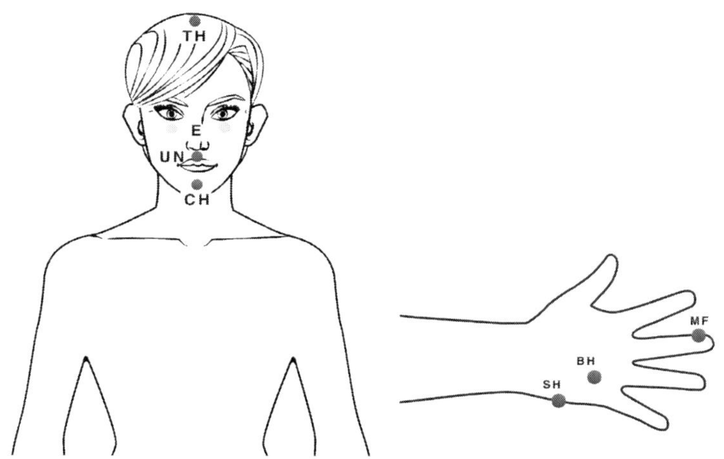

Tapping Points

TH	Top of Head
E	Under Eyes
UN	Under Nose
CH	Chin
MF	Middle Finger
BH	Back of Hand
B	Bilateral Brain Stimulation (not a point)
SH	Side of Hand

First Time Through

Think about any ways you have struggled with a lack of dreams or remembering your dreams and any recurring nightmares or bad dreams, while using your fingertips to tap 3-5 times on each point in the algorithm.

When you get to BH+B(30), tap the BH continuously while stepping back and forth or moving your eyes side to side for at least 30 seconds. The B stands for bilateral, so you are trying to get bilateral brain stimulation going by doing things that cross the vertical hemisphere of the body.

Second Time Through

After you've gone through the points focusing on lack of vision, go back through the points again focusing on having good dreams from God, inviting him to speak to you in this way.

Third Time Through

Meditate on this verse as you tap through the points a third time:

> *Then, after doing all those things, I will pour out my Spirit upon all people. Your sons and daughters will prophesy. Your old men will dream dreams, and your young men will see visions.*
>
> Joel 2:28 (NLT)

Repeat this tapping algorithm a few times a day, and especially before bed.

This Month's Tapping Video

URL and Password are both case sensitive

http://bit.ly/HebrewMonthsTapping
Password: RipeInEachSeason

Tevet טבת

Starts in December or January

The first of Tevet is when Esther was crowned queen (Esther 2:16). From the very beginning it is a month marked by authority. Tevet also marks the end of Hanukkah, the Feast of Dedication. On the 2nd of Tevet we light the last candle remembering God's provision of oil to keep the lampstand burning until more oil could be purified for use in the temple.

The word Hanukkah comes from the Hebrew verb meaning "to dedicate". While our modern celebration of Hanukkah resembles more of a Jewish version of a Christmas holiday celebration with gifts and other traditions, Hanukkah was originally a religious festival focused on remembering the Lord's miraculous provision and the restoration of Jewish authority over the temple and freedom from the enemies who had ruled over them.

Prophetically, Hanukkah speaks to the light each of us carry as Christians and the authority we have as the temples of the Holy Spirit.

> *Now you understand that I have imparted to you all my authority to trample over his kingdom. You will trample upon every demon before you and overcome every power Satan possesses. Absolutely nothing will be able to harm you as you walk in this authority. However, your real source of joy isn't merely that these spirits submit to your authority, but that your names are written in the journals of heaven and that you*

> *belong to God's kingdom. This is the true source of your authority.*
>
> Luke 10:19-20 (TPT)

As the verse cautions, it's important to not get caught up in a prideful authority — seeking to get revenge out of anger or bitterness. This month we are pressing into that godly authority that comes from our salvation and indwelling of the Holy Spirit.

This is a season to reject the lies that whisper, "*You are powerless*" and cling to the truth that we are truly powerful in Christ. Focus this month on taking authority over your emotions, dealing with the roots of pain, and bringing it all under submission to God.

The Tenth of Tevet, Asarah BiTevet, is a minor fast mourning the siege of Jerusalem by Nebuchadnezzar, which ultimately led to the destruction of Solomon's temple (2 Kings 25:1). For Israel, this siege also represented the loss of their authority over the land God had given them. According to Jubilees Tevet is also when Adam and

Eve were removed from the Garden of Eden (Genesis 3:24).

What has God given you that you have lost authority over? What promised lands have slipped away? Mourn the losses, repent for any way you've contributed to the loss, and ask God to restore the authority he intended for you to have.

In Matthew 17:21, Jesus explains to his disciples that some types of spiritual authority only come by a lifestyle of prayer and fasting; ask God to show you ways to begin growing in that type of authority as well.

With all of this focus on authority, it is important to remember we must stay centered in God's will as we operate in our God-given authority. Jesus had all authority in Heaven and Earth (Matthew 28:18), but he only did what he saw the Father doing, only said what he heard the Father saying (John 5:19-20).

In Genesis 18 angelic visitors came to Abraham (during Tevet according to Jubilees) telling him his wife Sarah would have a son within a year. A little over a decade prior Abraham and Sarah (then Abram and Sarai) longing for a child decided Abraham should have a child with Hagar (Genesis 16). This wasn't out of the ordinary for their culture. God had not yet told them Sarah beyond her fertile years would have a child. All Abraham knew was that God had told him his heirs would be as numerous as the stars, and so far, he had zero (Genesis 15). They went outside God's plan for Abraham's heirs and used their own authority and power to give him an heir. Over two-thousand years later we are still reaping the consequences of this decision with the strife between the offspring of Ishmael and the offspring of Isaac.

We can be outside God's plan and authority even when we are pursuing his promises. Especially in this season of authority, ask God to search your heart, to show you anywhere you are operating in your own authority and listen carefully for what he's saying, look closely for what he is doing.

The liver is associated with Tevet and often is connected to feelings of powerlessness, repression, condemnation, disappointment, indecisiveness, anger, and panic. This meridian is active from 1-3 a.m. so if you wake up at this time ask Holy Spirit what emotions are being triggered and pray to release them.

I'm praying for you this month that you break free from the bondage of lies that have kept you feeling powerless. May you be filled with full knowledge of your identity in Christ and the authority you have as a child of God.

Other Scripture References to Tevet

Genesis 3:24; 18; 19; 34; 46:28-30 (According to Jubilees)

2 Kings 25:1

1 Chronicles 27:13

Ezra 10:16

Esther 2:15-18

Jeremiah 39:1; 52:4

Ezekiel 24; 29; 33:21

Zechariah 8:19

Tevet Tapping

CTT Exercise for Authority:

TH - T - UN - R - MF - BH+B(30) - SH

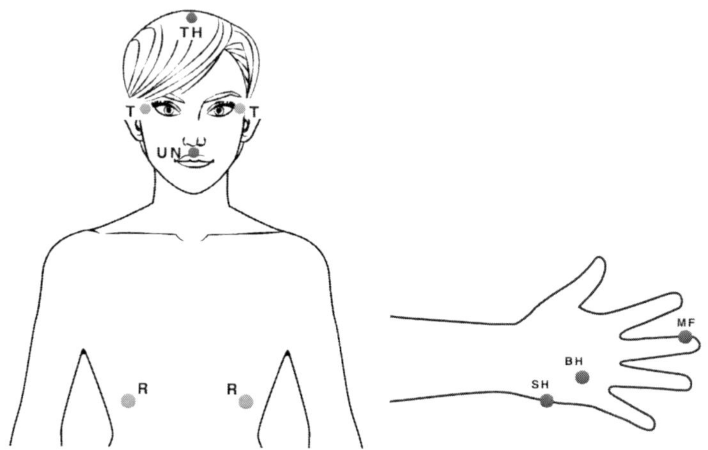

Tapping Points

TH	Top of Head
T	Temples
UN	Under Nose
R	Bottom of Ribcage
MF	Middle Finger
BH	Back of Hand
B	Bilateral Brain Stimulation (not a point)
SH	Side of Hand

First Time Through

Think about any ways you have struggled with feeling powerless or like you lack godly authority while using your fingertips to tap 3-5 times on each point in the algorithm.

When you get to BH+B(30), tap the BH continuously while stepping back and forth or moving your eyes side to side for at least 30 seconds. The B stands for bilateral, so you are trying to get bilateral brain stimulation going by doing things that cross the vertical hemisphere of the body.

Second Time Through

After you've gone through the points focusing on feeling powerless, go back through the points again focusing on being filled with godly authority and power.

Third Time Through

Meditate on this verse as you tap through the points a third time. This is a long one so it's a good time to use a reminder statement as you tap.

> *Now you understand that I have imparted to you all my authority to trample over his kingdom. You will trample upon every demon before you and overcome every power Satan possesses. Absolutely nothing will be able to harm you as you walk in this authority. However, your real source of joy isn't merely that these spirits submit to your authority, but that your names are written in the journals of heaven and that you belong to God's kingdom. This is the true source of your authority.*
>
> Luke 10:19-20 (TPT)

Repeat this tapping algorithm a few times a day, especially when you are feeling powerless.

This Month's Tapping Video

URL and Password are both case sensitive

http://bit.ly/HebrewMonthsTapping

Password: RipeInEachSeason

Shevat שבט

Starts in January or February

On the first of Shevat, in Deuteronomy chapter 1, Moses gave the Israelites the commands God has for them, including the initial command to take the promised land. The response to these commands shaped the trajectory of the next 40+ years of Israel. What was supposed to be a foundation of righteousness and a time to declare, "My blessings are on the way!" became a season of repeated doubts and disobedience, leading to a long season of wandering.

Fortunately for us, our foundation of righteousness is not built on our ability to obey the law; our foundation of righteousness is Jesus and our faith in him.

> *Not having a righteousness of my own that comes from the law, but that which comes through faith in Christ, the righteousness from God that depends on faith*
>
> Philippians 3:9 (ESV)

Shevat is also commonly associated with Leviticus 27:32-33 (HCSB)

> *Every tenth animal from the herd or flock, which passes under the shepherd's rod, will be holy to the Lord. He is not to inspect whether it is good or bad, and he is not to make a substitution for it. But if he does make a substitution, both the animal and its substitute will be holy.*

This seemingly boring verse about proper procedure for sacrifice is actually a powerful prophetic statement about our righteousness in Christ. In the Old Testament system of sacrifice if you wanted to exchange the dedicated animal for sacrifice for a different animal both animals would then be considered holy. Christ exchanged his death for ours, and in the process bestowed upon us his righteousness.

Another Levitical passage significant to Shevat is Leviticus 19:23-25 (NASB)

> *Now when you enter the land and plant all kinds of trees for food, then you shall count their fruit as forbidden. For three years it shall be forbidden to you; it shall not be eaten. And in the fourth year all its fruit shall be holy, an offering of praise to the Lord. But in the fifth year you shall eat its fruit, so that its yield may increase for you; I am the Lord your God.*

Tu BiShevat, which means he 15th of Shevat, is known as the "New Year for Trees" or Rosh HaShanah La'Ilanot. This is the day that is used to calculate the number of years since a tree was planted and take note of the indications of fruit expected in the coming season. Spiritually it is also a season to take inventory of what is planted in our lives, what is producing fruit? What will be ripe in due time? What good things do we need to abstain from because it is not yet their time? As Israel's decisions affected generations to come, our decisions and planning for the fruit in our lives can leave a legacy of blessing or cursing long after we pass away.

The New Year for Trees is also commonly a time of year when our relationships with food are reevaluated and fasting is used to deepen our hunger for the spiritual rather than the physical. Daniel's fast from the king's delicacies is sometimes associated with Shevat (Daniel 1:8-17). However, "fast" is somewhat of a misnomer in Daniel's story.

Daniel understood that God's law wasn't just about physical health, but that following his commands brought spiritual life as well. In this foreign land, stripped of his culture and identity, Daniel sought to remain faithful to God's commands even in what he ate. His abstention was an expression of his spiritual hunger, not a desire to deepen his hunger through fasting. "At the end of ten days their appearance seemed better, and they were fatter than all the youths who had been eating the king's choice food" (Daniel 1:15 NASB). Daniel and his friends clearly weren't starving or lacking anything to eat during their "fast". And we will not lack anything when we hunger for righteousness and stay in communion with the Holy Spirit.

For Shevat the body part is the gullet – or throat. It's unclear how well the organs in the throat were understood in ancient Jewish culture, but the thyroid is an organ that would make sense. The thyroid meridian is associated with feelings of rejection, vulnerability, mania, and being shut down. Often times, the gullet is often associated with our voice and feeling like we can express ourselves. The thyroid meridian is active from 9-11 p.m. so tapping as you wind down for bed is especially good this month.

I'm praying for you this month that you find a deeper assurance of your righteousness in Christ. That this firm foundation gives you freedom to pursue fruit and blessing from a place of abundance rather than one of works and law. *Your blessing is on the way!* Declare it throughout this month!

Other Scripture References to Shevat

Deuteronomy 1:3

1 Chronicles 27:14

Zechariah 1:7-20

Shevat Tapping

CTT Exercise for Righteousness:

EB – E – A – TB – BH+B(30) – SH

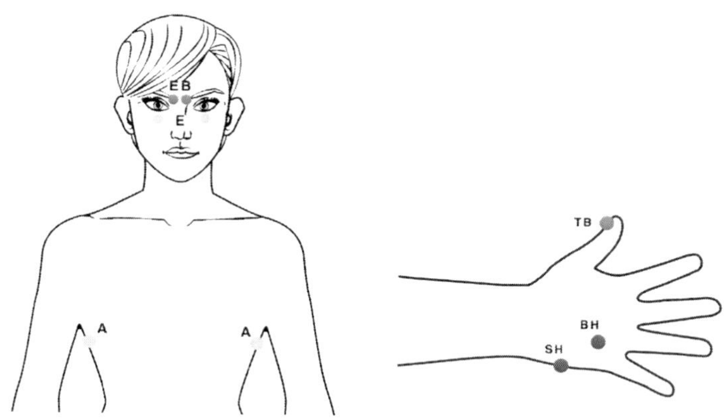

Tapping Points

EB	Eyebrows
E	Under Eyes
A	Under Arms
TB	Thumb
BH	Back of Hand
B	Bilateral Brain Stimulation (not a point)
SH	Side of Hand

First Time Through

Think about any ways you have struggled with feeling the righteousness you have in Christ or struggled with faith while using your fingertips to tap 3-5 times on each point in the algorithm.

When you get to BH+B(30), tap the BH continuously while stepping back and forth or moving your eyes side to side for at least 30 seconds. The B stands for bilateral, so you are trying to get bilateral brain stimulation going by doing things that cross the vertical hemisphere of the body.

Second Time Through

After you've gone through the points focusing areas of struggle, go back through the points again focusing on being filled with your righteousness in Christ, full of faith.

Third Time Through

Meditate on this verse as you tap through the points a third time:

Not having a righteousness of my own that comes from the law, but that which comes through faith in Christ, the righteousness from God that depends on faith.

Philippians 3:9 (ESV)

Repeat this tapping algorithm a few times a day, especially when you are feeling a lack of faith and confidence in your righteousness through Christ.

This Month's Tapping Video

URL and Password are both case sensitive

http://bit.ly/HebrewMonthsTapping
Password: RipeInEachSeason

Adar אדר

Starts in February or March

Adar is the month that Esther fasted and prayed for the Jewish people when Haman plotted genocide to wipe them out. It's the month that the Jewish people were not only spared, but those who wished to harm them were hung in the very gallows meant to do the harm. Adar is a season for the decrees made against you to be broken, and your enemies to reap the very plots they made against you.

The Jewish holiday Purim is celebrated on the 14th of the month. Purim is means "lots" and celebrates that the lots cast against the Jewish people by Haman were overturned. Sometimes Purim is thought of a Jewish Halloween with the costumes and masks that are worn at this celebration. These masks symbolize the hidden identity of Esther and the pain of having to mask our identities and joy. Ultimately Esther's mask provided her the influence to save her people and allow them all to celebrate with unmasked joy.

What we often miss about Esther's story is the time it took to play out. It is a full year from Esther 3 when Haman issues his decree that the Jews are to be killed, to Esther 8-9 when Mordecai issues his decree, the Jews are empowered to defend themselves, and Haman is hung on his own gallows.

Another long wait fulfilled this month was the dedication of the Second Temple. As explained in the Elul chapter, the foundations of the temple sat for seventeen years before the work began again and it took four years to complete once the work was restarted. The second temple was dedicated on the 3rd of Adar (Ezra 6:13-18). Aligning with Jeremiah's prophecy (Jeremiah 25:11-12; 29:10), it took twenty-one years since the return from exile and seventy years from the destruction of the First Temple before the completion and the dedication of the Second Temple.

While we have looked at the themes each month individually, Adar highlights the importance of seeing the layered whole of how God works throughout the seasons. Our God is "the God of the suddenly", but often there is a long wait until that "suddenly". Keep an eye this month for long awaited breakthroughs.

This is a season for you to operate in your true identity and be released into joy, a time for worry, despair, and depression to bend their knee to the supernatural resources, protection, and celebration. Purim also marks the schemes of your enemy being defeated. Pay attention to the spiritual battles you are facing in this season. You may notice a shift after Purim.

In John 5 Purim is mentioned as a Jewish festival that Jesus attended prior to Passover. It was during this festival that Jesus healed the lame man laying by the pool at Bethesda. The man had lain by this healing pool many years yet never had stepped into the pool because he had no one to help him get off his mat.

Jesus told him to pick up his mat and walk, so he did. Since this took place on the Sabbath, people confronted the man telling him it wasn't allowed for him to be healed on this day. The man told them to take it up with Jesus and went on enjoying his healing. This is a season to cling to what we know God has given us or told us and let the naysayers take it up with him.

Adar is also the month when Jesus told Peter to get a coin out of a fish's mouth to pay their taxes (Matthew 17:27). It's a season of supernatural provision breaking through into our natural needs. Take time this month to reflect in gratitude on the ways you have already seen supernatural provision and keep your eyes peeled for supernatural solutions to the natural problems you are facing.

Some years we get a double-portion of all things Adar. As explained in the "A Different Kind of Time" chapter, similar to the leap day used in the solar Gregorian calendar, the lunisolar Hebrew calendar uses the leap month of a second Adar. The Hebrew leap years follow a Metonic cycle, meaning that leap years occur seven times within a nineteen-year cycle. This works out to about every two-three years on years 3, 6, 8, 11, 14, 17, and 19. In 2022 we are in the eleventh year of the Metonic cycle.

Adar is associated with the spleen. Likely not an organ you think about much, but it's associated with feelings of anxiety, compulsivity, apathy, despair, and stress. The spleen meridian is active from 9-11 a.m. so be extra sure to fill up with joy in the morning.

I'm praying for you this month that you feel free to remove the masks that have hidden your true identity. That you no longer have to hide your joy in fear of pain, but can celebrate freely with supernatural joy.

Other Scripture References to Adar

Exodus 9:18-35

Leviticus 8 (According to Jasher)

2 Kings 25:27

1 Chronicles 27:15

Ezra 6:13-18

Esther 3:7, 13; 8:12; 9:1, 20-32

Jeremiah 52:31

Ezekiel 32:1

Matthew 2:19

Adar Tapping

CTT Exercise for Joy:

UN – CH – A – TB – BH+B(30) – SH

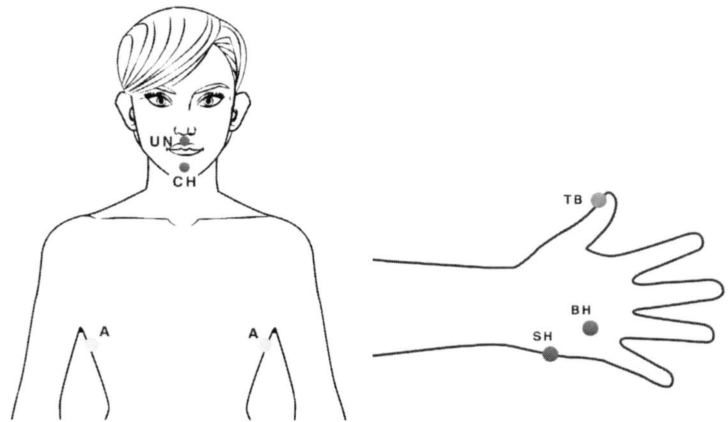

Tapping Points

UN Under Nose
CH Chin
A Under Arms
TB Thumb
BH Back of Hand
B Bilateral Brain Stimulation (not a point)
SH Side of Hand

First Time Through

Think about any way you feel a lack of joy - loss, grief, sadness, or despair, while using your fingertips to tap 3-5 times on each point in the algorithm.

When you get to BH+B(30), tap the BH continuously while stepping back and forth or moving your eyes side to side for at least 30 seconds. The B stands for bilateral, so you are trying to get bilateral brain stimulation going by doing things that cross the vertical hemisphere of the body.

Second Time Through

After you've gone through the points focusing on feeling a lack of joy go back through the points again focusing on feeling filled with joy - all obstacles to joy removed, no fear of joy being stolen.

Third Time Through

Meditate on this verse as you tap through the points a third time:

> *For you will go out in joy, be led home in peace. And as you go the land itself will break out in cheers; The mountains and the hills will erupt in song, and the trees of the field will clap their hands.*
>
> Isaiah 55:12 (VOICE)

Repeat this tapping algorithm a few times a day, especially when you are struggling with feeling a lack of joy.

This Month's Tapping Video

URL and Password are both case sensitive

http://bit.ly/HebrewMonthsTapping
Password: RipeInEachSeason

Enjoy the book?

Help others find it by writing a review!

I just tried tapping for the first time and I felt ridiculous but in no time I was bawling and worshipping Jesus! Thank you so much for sharing this book with me!"

Laura

"Full of lovely surprises each month. I've found many unexpected perspectives as the time in scripture is matched to emotions with excellent ideas and tapping exercises to heal and grow by."

Jane

Your Name!

I am getting so much revelation and healing from the knowledge in this book!"

CKH

If you're interested in health from a Spirit lead, God approach, this will hold some missing pieces to that puzzle!"

Desarae

Continue the Healing

Three authors, three books, continue the series to go even deeper into the layered significance of the Hebrew months!

Hebrew calendar, blog posts, t-shirts, mugs, monthly subscriptions, and more all available on the Healing in the Hebrew Months website.

www.HealingintheHebrewMonths.com

Healing can happen at any time, but certain seasons are more open for healing in specific areas of our lives. There are special things God wants to bring forth in every season that will propel us forward into our destinies.

Connect with Community

Join the Healing in the Hebrew Months Facebook Group to connect with other like-minded believers!

www.healinginthehebrewmonths.com/community

Recommended Resources

His Appointed Times by Christine Vales

Celebrating Jesus in the Biblical Feasts by Dr. Richard Booker

Jewish New Testament Commentary by David H. Stern

Follow the Rabbi teaching series by Ray Vander Laan

Chronological Study Bible

About the Author

Leah Lesesne (pronounced lay-uh luh-sane) delights in connecting with God through the Jewish roots of Christianity and the spiritual rhythms he set in motion. She spent years in the mental health counseling world frustrated by the lack of lasting healing she saw. She knew there had to be better answers for the pain her clients felt. Convinced of God's promise in 1 Thessalonians 5:23 of complete wholeness spirit-mind-body, she returned to her roots of inner healing prayer and found revelation after revelation of God's answers to lasting breakthrough. Her mission is to share those revelations to help you be as healthy, whole, and close to Jesus as possible.

Leah and her family live in Atlanta, GA with their urban farm full of critters. When she's not writing you can find her out in her garden with a good book and a cup of tea, or chasing a wayward chicken.

Find her online:

www.captivethoughttherapy.com
www.HealingintheHebrewMonths.com
www.facebook.com/shelemahwellness
www.instagram.com/shelemahwellness

Other Books by the Author

Miracles & Dedication: Christian Devotions for the Festival of Lights

Out of 400 years of silence burst a prophetic miracle of provision and light. What if there is a deeper meaning to the Festival of Lights for Christians today? Can we celebrate both Hanukkah and Christmas?
Illuminate the Christian symbolism found in Hanukkah as you explore the history of the holiday, how Jesus celebrated it, and the themes of miracles and dedication.

Eight nightly devotions include:

- Blessings to declare as you light the candles
- Readings from the traditional Jewish schedule and from the New Testament
- Questions for reflection and discussion
- Guided prayers to engage with what you learned

Perfect for the holiday season, this short devotional will give you a new perspective of Hanukkah and help prepare your heart for celebrating the Light of the World's birth at Christmas.

Every Thought Captive

11 Christian Tapping Exercises for Emotional Freedom

Keep on tapping! Eleven CTT tapping exercises like the monthly tapping exercises in this book plus a general emotional exercise, and exercises for forgiveness and getting your head and heart to agree on truth, plus an emotional synonyms chart to help you pick an exercise to tap with and grow your emotional vocabulary.

Captive Thought Therapy Workbook

Walk Yourself through Emotional and Spiritual Healing. This workbook for personal use includes 40 more individual emotion exercises like the ones in this book, the general exercise, exercises for forgiveness and getting your head and heart to agree on truth and an emotional synonyms chart to help you pick an exercise and expand your emotional vocabulary!

Healthy & Whole: 60 Days to Complete Wellness

Part devotional, part health challenge, *Healthy & Whole* will take you on a sixty-day journey to complete wellness, body-mind-spirit. By building new physical, emotional, and spiritual lifestyles rather than just new habits you will find your unique path to being as healthy, whole, and close to Jesus as possible.

Body Coaching: 30 Days of Spirit Led Weight Loss

"Body, we need to talk..."

What we say to ourselves and about ourselves matters. Body coaching is a 30-day program of positive self-talk. Taking authority in our spirits over our bodies and giving ourselves the pep talks we've desperately needed.

It's not about will powering your way through another diet or exercise program, it's about partnering your body, mind, and spirit together so that you can experience the breakthroughs you've been longing for.